WHAT PEOPLE ARE S
SAFEST PLACE

Retired Army Chaplain Paul Linzey has written a revealing and moving "real life" book about chaplain ministry. His amazing experiences essentially provide a powerful textbook for anyone desiring to know what a military chaplain does in war. With passion and love he displays a chaplain's daily opportunities to share his faith, listen, coach, mentor, advise, preach, teach and provide comfort and hope for war-weary Soldiers, all of which confirmed his Call to be a pastor, chaplain, teacher, and Army officer. A VERY good book!

Chaplain, Brigadier General, Douglas E. Lee, US Army (Ret.)
Former Assistant Chief of Chaplains for Mobilization
Previous Military Chaplain Endorsing Agent
Presbyterian and Reformed Commission on
Chaplains & Military Personnel

Safest Place in Iraq clearly shows the incarnational ministry of the chaplain. Chaplain Linzey's presence with his soldiers, living out his faith, and ministering to those service members and others in the name of the Lord demonstrated this incarnational ministry. I was constantly reminded of two things in this book: the ministry of presence by the chaplain and the constant protection of the "shadow of God" that David the Psalmist wrote about in the Soldier's Psalm, Psalm 91.

This is a book I highly recommend, and will recommend to my students working toward their Master of Divinity to become military chaplains.

Chaplain, Colonel, Keith Travis, US Army (Ret.)
Professor of Chaplaincy at Rawlings Divinity School, Liberty University
Former Faith Group Endorser, Southern Baptist Convention

If you start reading *Safest Place in Iraq*, you won't put it down. Chaplain Paul Linzey's account of deployment in Iraq provides amazing insights about how God works in the lives of people stationed together on a small forward operating base in Iraq during a very dangerous time. As a former active duty chaplain and denominational endorser, I especially recommend this book for military chaplains and those training to become military chaplains. A true masterpiece!

Chaplain, Colonel, Scott McChrystal, US Army (Ret.)
Author of Daily Strength for the Battle series,
Managing Editor of The Warriors Bible
Former Military & VA Chaplain Endorsing Agent,
Assemblies of God

Gripping . . . compelling . . . the story of a calling from God and the indelible mark of true faith. Having known Chaplain Paul Linzey since his first day in the Army, he tells his remarkable story of finding God's grace in the midst of war in Iraq. Paul's story will bless you and help you realize that no matter where you are, or whatever challenges you face, trusting in God is the "Safest Place."

Chaplain, Colonel, Ronald A. Casteel, US Army (Ret.)
Former Command Chaplain, U.S. Army Reserve Command

This power-packed memoir by Chaplain Linzey has brought the realities of war from somewhere in the small headlines to the front page of our consciousness. *Safest Place in Iraq* proves to us that even in war, God is still there and not silent, doing miracles and using relationships to change lives, reminding us that He is not only relevant in the pew, but also on the battlefield.

Chaplain, Lieutenant Colonel, Bill Hartman, US Army (Ret.)
Pastoral Care Coordinator at Deltona Alliance Church, Deltona, FL

When Paul Linzey deployed, he asked our inner-city church to track with him and pray for him. The people in our congregation spend their lives on a different sort of battlefield but one just as dire, and they still strongly resonated with Paul's life and death ministry over there. For a number of years, the Lord granted me the privilege of serving under him as my supervising chaplain. The Paul you meet in his book is identical to the one I knew: a man who imitates Jesus as naturally as he inhales and exhales oxygen. A Godly ease about Paul pervades this crisply written, engrossing narrative—a constant, spontaneous knowing of exactly what to do whatever the circumstance.

Long before I became a chaplain and a Christian, I was a spiritually despairing combat officer in Vietnam. I would have given anything to have had Paul Linzey as my chaplain. *Safest Place in Iraq* is so well written and so accurate in its depiction of war and what comes after. I couldn't put it down.

Chaplain, Lieutenant Colonel, Jack LaPietra, US Army Reserve (Ret.) *Pastor, New Life in Christ Church, Lakewood, CO*

You'll be drawn into this book from the first page. Colonel Linzey takes you into battle with him and gives you an amazing perspective about service to the Lord while at war. His accounts are nothing like you see or hear from news reports, but candid and real stories about the people he served with overseas. You will read about Pastor James, the miracle when a Ukrainian solider was saved, and Mac, a cop from Philadelphia who only wanted a Bible of his own, and finally saw Jesus in a new way. These accounts will draw you in, and you will not want to stop reading this book. I'm honored to call Colonel Linzey my friend and owe him a debt of gratitude for his service. I was in awe with the way he handled the challenges of war and promoted the Lord. *Safest Place in Iraq* will leave a lasting impression and give you a deeper appreciation for our men and women in the armed services, and how God always provides. Bravo Paul.

Del Duduit, *Author of* Buckeye Believer *and*
Dugout Devotions

Paul is a great chaplain and man of God. It is clear from this book that he has been used much by God in the lives of so many Soldiers. I am included in that list, and am proud to call Paul my friend and a mentor. I recommend Paul's book, *Safest Place in Iraq*, as a testimony to how God used a humble man in reaching so many with His love.

Chaplain, Lieutenant Colonel, Mike DuCharme,
US Army

It's easy to wonder where God is when the world breaks out in war. Tragedies often make people question the love of God or even the existence of God. But Colonel Paul Linzey makes it very clear that even in the greatest uncertainties of life, God makes a difference for those who turn to Him. With clarity and relevant detail, Colonel Linzey takes the reader into the day to day of military life in a war zone and shares what the news media does not. It became obvious to me in reading *Safest Place in Iraq* that Colonel Linzey was in the middle of the Iraq war by divine appointment. The lives he touched for Jesus Christ were given the opportunity to be changed for a lifetime, and many accepted that opportunity.

I found this book to be very interesting and inspiring. It shares the emotional ups and downs of living with the threat of injury or death. It gives insight into the struggle many of our soldiers faced during that war. For me, I was personally challenged anew to start each day seeking God's direction in how He may want to use me through the course of that day. For those of us wanting to make a spiritual difference in the lives of others, the "friendship follows ministry" slogan was a great reminder of how to be effective.

I highly recommend *Safest Place in Iraq* as a challenge and encouragement to living for God in difficult times.

Jim Ayers, Retired Pastor and District Official,
Assemblies of God

Great story. Powerful narrative on the conflicting forces experienced by Chaplains who are committed husbands/fathers. So necessary for everyone to hear – especially Chaplains who think they must be super-human to be pastoral. The writing jumps out such that I could see the movements, hear the mortars, feel the love & crisis fear, experience the emotions of personal ministry. Captivating!

Chaplain, Lieutenant Colonel, Steven O. Langehough,
US Army (Ret.) *PhD, Licensed Alcohol & Drug Counselor*
Executive Director, Arms of Agape, Inc.,
Getting Back on Track Counseling

In this book, *Safest Place in Iraq*, Colonel Paul E. Linzey, Chaplain, US Army (Ret.) gives a first-hand view of life on the front lines. Knowing he could have remained safely in the US, Chaplain Linzey chose to enter harm's way to minister life to those who face death every day. He speaks of depression, defeat, and death; but also of laughter, liberty, and life. Each chapter is its own intriguing story; but together they tell of drama, mystery, inner struggles, fear – yet undying loyalty to each other. Soldiers risk their lives, and some give their lives, to support and defend life and liberty – even in Iraq. The book will take mere hours to read, yet what you read will change your life.

S. Eugene Linzey: *Author, Speaker, Mentor*
Former Pastor of Christian Family Church, Taos, NM
Former President of Siloam Springs Writers Guild,
Siloam Springs, AR

Chaplain Paul Linzey has written a fascinating and compelling book, recounting his time of ministry in Iraq. Once you start reading it you will want to be able to read it in one sitting. Throughout this war, everyone was riveted to their televisions watching the chaos and bloodshed, but what was not seen on the networks was how God was working and using military Chaplains to serve the force in the most critical moments of their lives. This book does an amazing job of opening a window, revealing to us that God was actively working in what some would mistakenly call "a god forsaken region." Make sure you have lots of time to read if you pick up *Safest Place in Iraq*.

Chaplain, Colonel, Mack Griffith, US Army (Ret.)
Associate Endorser for the Presbyterian and Reformed
Commission on Chaplains

Safety is a scarce commodity in a warzone. With the help of chaplains like Colonel Paul "Chaps" Linzey, soldiers learn that safety is an internal presence, independent of their location and body armor. This book takes you through the journey of finding peace in the chaos of war. A must read for every person experiencing a loved one's deployment.

Among a deployed soldier's most precious treasures are the rare feelings of peace and security. *Safest Place in Iraq* shares the journey of discovery experienced by one dedicated Army chaplain and those he served. This book is a must read for those warriors and their families who are deployed or preparing for a deployment. Warzones aren't noted for their safety and comfort. As General William Tecumseh Sherman stated "… War is hell." The Safest Place in Iraq takes you on the journey of how one small base in central Iraq found its way to God's grace through the efforts of one of God's most humble servants.

J. D. Wininger, Christian Author, Former USSOCOM Operator

What kind of person volunteers to go to war? Who signs up to engage in a level of suffering and pain that few will ever observe first-hand? Colonel Paul Linzey certainly loves his country, but there is something else that drives him into the trenches of human need. As I turned the pages of this book, I was moved by a real man, telling a real story, about a real God. The story of Daniel and the lion's den feels mythical when we approach the text out of mundane duty. However, Colonel Linzey awakens our imagination as he reacquaints the reader with the ancient city, Babylon. We are reminded of the humanity in every biblical hero and modern-day soldier. Each must confront fear and anxiety at a deep, gut level. In moments of doubt and questioning, a word from God that echoes in a believer's heart brings more security and courage than a powerful army at Camp Echo. Thank you, Colonel. You have reminded us to be faithful to the call of God. There is no better place serve, than the place where God calls, even if that place is near Babylon.

Dr. Mark J. Anthony, *Lead Pastor of Trinity Church & School, Sharpsburg, GA*

Safest Place in Iraq

SAFEST PLACE IN IRAQ

EXPERIENCING GOD DURING WAR

COLONEL PAUL LINZEY
US Army Chaplain (RET.)

NASHVILLE

NEW YORK • LONDON • MELBOURNE • VANCOUVER

SAFEST PLACE IN IRAQ

EXPERIENCING GOD DURING WAR

Published in New York, New York, by Morgan James Publishing. Morgan James is a trademark of Morgan James, LLC. www.MorganJamesPublishing.com

To protect the privacy of the people in the stories, most of the names have been omitted, and others have been changed

Unless otherwise noted, all Scripture quotations are taken from the HCSB®, Copyright © 1999, 2000, 2002, 2003, 2009 by Holman Bible Publishers. Used by permission.

HCSB® is a federally registered trademark of Holman Bible Publishers
ISBN 9781642799170 paperback
ISBN 9781642799187 eBook
Library of Congress Control Number: 2019954759

Cover and Interior Design by:
Chris Treccani
www.3dogcreative.net

Cover Photo by:
Paul Linzey

Author's website/blog: https://paullinzey.com

Morgan James is a proud partner of Habitat for Humanity Peninsula and Greater Williamsburg. Partners in building since 2006.

Get involved today! Visit
MorganJamesPublishing.com/giving-back

DEDICATIONS

To the men and women who lived, served, fought, and died in Iraq:
Military and civilian, American and Coalition Forces

To Master Sergeant Rosita France: Chaplain Assistant, ministry
partner, and friend, who saved my life, then was forced to
return to the States because of a war-related injury

To those whose stories are included here, and those who
participated in the religious services at Camp Echo

To the men of the 0800 Military Transition Team

To John Reno, whose gyroscope guided the
Eye-in-the-Sky that saved my life

And to my granddaughter, Annalise,
born the day I left to go to Iraq

TABLE OF CONTENTS

FOREWORD

I have served in the ministry for the past 40 years, either as a senior pastor of a church, the president of a seminary, or the president of a non-profit. I have authored books and spoken in numerous nations. I have addressed diverse audiences and ministered in some unusual settings.

However, I have never been awakened in the middle of the night by an air raid siren warning me to scramble to the nearest bomb shelter in order to survive the onslaught of incoming rockets. I have encouraged congregants in the morning before they went to work. But I have never spoken to people moments before they embarked on a journey that would put them in the path of IEDs and sniper fire. I have often left my wife and children behind when traveling to out-of-town speaking engagements. But I have never had to say goodbye to them before departing on a six-month tour of duty. As a pastor, I visited people in the hospital. But I never visited anyone who had just had his legs blown off. I have answered to congregational committees and trustee boards. But my ministry has never been supervised by a non-Christian colonel or general. Throughout the years, I have ministered to people who belong to a wide variety of Christian denominations. But I have never ministered to people from more than a dozen denominations *at the same time.*

Whenever I think my ministry has been challenging, I consider the many military chaplains I know. I have had the privilege of ministering to military chaplains for more than a dozen years. They are some of the finest servants of God I have ever met.

I was delighted to read *Safest Place in Iraq* by Paul Linzey. He provides a compelling, vivid, and inspirational account of his experience serving as a chaplain at Camp Echo deep in Iraq. Facing the constant danger of rockets plummeting into his mile-wide encampment and ministering to soldiers who were in imminent danger, Linzey discovered the difference God's presence can make in one of the most dangerous places on Earth.

This book is riveting for numerous reasons. The ubiquitous threat of rockets, IEDs, and snipers leave the reader perennially on edge. The fundamental life questions that arise among people who are facing lethal danger is engaging. Linzey's descriptions of the wide assortment of people huddled together in that danger zone make for edge-of-your-seat reading.

Linzey doesn't write as an armchair theorist at a military school in America. Rather, he provides a candid and honest first-hand account of real-life ministry to people who desperately need it. You may have watched news stories about war zones on television, but you have likely never heard the kind of stories detailed on these pages. You may be a minister or engaged in Christian service in your local church, but it is doubtful you have faced the challenges Linzey encountered.

I encourage you to read this book prayerfully, thoughtfully, and humbly. Just be sure you don't start reading until you have ample time, because you won't want to put this book down.

Dr. Richard Blackaby

President of Blackaby Ministries International, Co-author of Experiencing God *and* Experiencing God Day-By-Day

Chapter 1

Heat, Danger, Dust, and Death

W hen they told me where I was going, they said it was the *Safest Place in Iraq*, but by the time I got there, things had changed. On a Tuesday night, the dining facility was crowded, bustling, with hardly an empty chair, when mortars landed on the building. Of the more than two hundred people in the dining facility (DFAC), eighteen were killed. Forty-seven were wounded, some seriously, but they'd survive—with or without that arm or leg or eye.

People were stunned, walking around like zombies. Most avoided eating in the DFAC, even after it was repaired and they started serving meals again. From that moment, incoming mortars and rockets became part of the routine that was soon to be my daily life.

Located on the main rail line between Baghdad and Basra, Diwaniyah is known for its manufacturing, and famous for its automobile tires. Dust-colored high-rise apartment buildings line the streets, each building home to more than a thousand people. Water from the Euphrates River irrigates the farms and groves outside the city, making the region one of the nation's most fertile.

Men from Diwaniyah would drive to a vacant field on the edge of town, bringing their rockets and mortars to fire at us. They did this in the morning on their way to work. Sometimes it was mid-day during a lunch break, and other times in the evening on their way home from work. Occasionally it was in the middle of the night. Some of the people shooting at us were teens or even younger. Often, they would launch their missiles-of-death just before, or right after their prayers.

Camp Echo was a small, roundish Forward Operating Base (FOB), about a mile in diameter, in the middle of the desert, with temperatures ranging from 110–120 degrees. The dirt, sand, and heat were inescapable. Every day began with a new film of dust on each desk, table, chair, bed, and floor. The layer of dirt thickened as the day wore on.

Surrounding the entire FOB was a 12-foot high concrete wall. The other side of the barrier consisted of dry fields inhabited by rabbits, snakes, and camel spiders. There were also scorpions, an occasional wild dog, and, of course, the men and boys trying to kill us.

I volunteered to go. My philosophy as an Army chaplain was that I wanted to be wherever soldiers had to go, and if they were at war, I wanted to be there with them. Not because I enjoy fighting. We all know that a chaplain is a non-combatant. I wasn't there to fight.

I was there to encourage, counsel, and pray; provide worship opportunities, friendship, and guidance; nurture the living, care for the wounded, and honor the dead; and guarantee the constitutional freedom of worship to men and women of all faiths, and the same freedom to men and women of no faith. Camp Echo was my home, my parish, my fiery furnace.

The day I arrived in March 2007, I met the commander: a pleasant, graying fifty-nine-year-old from Illinois who wanted to survive, go home to his wife, and retire to a life of fishing with his grandchildren. He told me our troops' morale was horrible, and that part of my job as the chaplain was to encourage them to stop grumbling and complaining. Several weeks later, when I walked into his office to check on a few things, he started spewing out his own frustration and anger.

"We're sitting ducks inside this FOB," he shouted, "and the General refuses to let us shoot. If I had my way, we'd put snipers in each tower along the wall, and whenever someone shows up with mortars and rockets, shoot 'im dead. I'm tired of sitting here doing nothing."

"Sir, my job is to help put an end to the grumbling."

He looked at me, paused, and laughed, remembering his own words, then continued griping. Even the Colonel needed someone safe to vent to, someone who would listen, someone who cared. It was a miserable place to be, and a terrible time to be there.

One morning, a mortar made a direct hit on the housing unit of one of the female civilians who worked at the FOB. A vibrant thirty-five-year-old from Houston, she was smart, pretty, popular, and dead. Seventy-five of our civilian workers packed up and went home the next day. They liked the job and the money, some of them earning more than $100,000 each year they worked in Iraq. In a few years they could make enough to fulfill several dreams and goals, but they didn't want to die. The fact that they could pick up and leave was wonderful for them, but awful for the soldiers. We didn't have that option.

I knew from the start that I could be wounded or killed. It was a weird feeling, and I came to accept it. How or when, I had no idea. But every time there was another explosion, I wondered if this was the day.

My wife also knew I might not make it home alive. Or if I did return, I might be a broken man–crippled, blind, psychologically damaged, or all of the above. With that possibility in mind, she told me before I left home, "I don't want to find out after you get back or after you're dead that you were in danger. I want to know right away."

The phrase "I want to know" describes much more than how she felt about what happened to her husband during the war. It's true about everything she does. She loves learning, is an avid reader, is addicted to research, and always wants to know more about everything. She might not have invented the internet, but it was certainly invented for her. She probably hasn't read every book in the world, but I would bet there's not an important book in the world she hasn't read or skimmed or at least knows something about. When I was heading to Iraq, she was writing her doctoral dissertation and preparing for a new teaching position. So, to hear her say "I want to know," elicited my response, "Oh yeah? What else is new?"

Many of our military personnel won't tell their spouse and family what they're going through during war, thinking they're protecting them. Plus, we're limited in what we're allowed to say or write to our families. But I have a hunch there are many, like my wife, who are better off knowing what's going on, and who want to know.

The first time I mentioned during a phone call some of the dangerous things that were happening, she said, "I already know. I saw it on TV and in the newspaper. They're mentioning Diwaniyah and Camp Echo by name." She scanned and sent me an *LA Times* article. I took it to our staff meeting the next morning, and discovered that many on our leadership team didn't know what was going on outside the wire.

Rockets and mortars exploding all over the FOB weren't the only danger, though. My busiest times were in the afternoons and evenings, so I got in the habit of exercising in the morning, sometimes on a treadmill in the gym, and sometimes outdoors. I went to the track one morning and discovered a group of people huddled toward one end of the oval. A nineteen-year-old soldier from a small town in Pennsylvania died of heatstroke while running. The temperature was about a hundred twenty degrees. He had returned from the States the night before.

While at home for his two-week mid-deployment R&R, he took his girlfriend out to dinner and proposed to her. She screamed "Yes," put on her shiny new engagement ring, and was eager for him to finish the deployment, come home, get married, and live happily ever after. Nineteen-year-old men aren't supposed to die like that.

Heat, danger, dust, and death formed the context for the job I was sent to do. Operating from the philosophy that "ministry follows friendship," I built relationships among the men and women at Camp Echo: military, civilian, American, and Coalition. This allowed me to be there when they were at their best and when they were at their worst, in their strongest moments and in their weakest.

In the heat of the battle and the heat of the desert, hours turn into days, which transition to nights, and add up to weeks and

CHAPTER 2

Unexpected Partners

There hadn't been a chaplain at Camp Echo during the three years the FOB had been in operation, but now that people were being wounded and some were dying, our leaders decided to send a chaplain. My job was to build a religious program from scratch, take care of the spiritual needs of the people, and provide a "ministry of presence." To do that, I needed a ministry team. I already had four congregations of prayer partners back in the States. Now I needed "boots on the ground" partners.

My first day at the FOB, somebody told me there was a civilian worker on post who was a pastor before the war. A Baptist preacher from North Carolina, James had been leading a Bible study every Sunday morning for the past year. In essence, he had been the only pastoral presence for the people at Camp Echo.

James worked the night shift, so on Friday night, the day after I arrived, I went looking for him and found him in his office around eleven p.m. A forty-two-year-old African American, he was a trim five-foot-nine with a ready smile, slight mustache, and graying goatee. He had a gold front tooth, which sometimes gleamed and sometimes was dark, depending on the lighting.

When I walked into his office, he was sitting at his desk. In front of him were two computers, a stack of paperback Bibles, water bottle, calculator, flashlight, thesaurus, telephone, and a fly swatter: things he considered essential. He wore a blue jacket with a hood. I never saw him without that jacket on, no matter how hot it was. He was indeed an ordained Baptist minister, and had heard that a "real chaplain" was coming.

When he saw that I was the new chaplain, he looked at me and grinned, flashing that gold tooth, but he was serious. The first words I heard him say were, "You gonna fire me since you're a real chaplain an' I'm not?"

I've read a lot of books and articles on various leadership styles and principles, and could easily make a case for asking James to step away from his previous role in the chapel program. It's a common practice, for example, to bring in an entirely different team when a new leader arrives. Another issue is that a lot of pastors and chaplains want to do all the ministry: preaching, teaching the Bible study, praying for people, and visiting the sick.

But I know how important it is for all God's people to be involved in ministry. Plus, I had a good feeling about the man, and I wanted to honor him for his faithfulness over the past year of leading the Bible study and praying for people.

So I said, "Pastor James, I have no intention of firing you. You were here ministering when there was no chaplain. Chances are, you might be here after I'm gone. How would you feel about us working together as co-pastors?"

When I called him Pastor James, his eyes opened big and he got excited. "Are you serious?"

"Yes, I'm serious. There's plenty to do. You already know everybody on post. You've been doing the job of pastor when nobody else was here. Perhaps you could show me around and introduce me to people in the various offices and sections."

"I can do that," James offered.

"And if the war continues, there might be times I have to be at the clinic or visiting another FOB when it's time for church. I think it's better if we worked as a team. What do you say? I could use your help."

"I like that plan," he said.

When I held out my hand to shake his, he threw his arms around me for a long hug, instead. "What about this Sunday morning?" he asked.

"Why don't you plan and lead the worship service, and then introduce me as the new chaplain, and I'll preach," I suggested. "At the end of the worship service, we'll serve communion side by side."

"That'll work."

"Then we'll take it week by week," I continued. "There's a lot to do, and we can accomplish more if we work together."

"Gotta deal." He showed off that gold tooth again.

The differences between us were obvious: different denominations, different personalities, different spiritual gifts, different skin color, and more. But the fact that we worked together, supported one another, and honored each other had an immediate impact on the people at Camp Echo. Just as important, it seemed the Lord was pleased with the way we handled things, and he blessed our efforts from day one.

In addition to having an experienced minister like Pastor James to work with, one Sunday morning, two female soldiers from the Motor Pool showed up for church.

"We hear your Chaplain Assistant had to go home."

"Yeah, she did," I replied. "She was an amazing NCO and Chaplain Assistant, but was injured on the job and went back to the States for surgery."

One of the two continued. "MSG France was awesome. She's the one who told us you were doing church. Well, since she's gone, we're here to volunteer as your new assistants."

They were a fantastic pair of ministry partners: always there, always early, always joyful. One of them told me, "My daddy's a pastor back home. I grew up in the church, so I know the ropes. We can do anything you need help with."

She was right. Both of them were sharp, spiritually minded, and experienced in church ministries. They could do it all.

The way things were shaping up, the Lord was providing a ministry team to cover for the absence of my Chaplain Assistant. First was Pastor James, and now these two assistants. It was like having a whole pastoral staff right there in the desert. I wasn't a lone wolf, trying to be-all, know-all, do-all. There were people in place who were ready to help, pray, advise, and share the load.

The decision to have Pastor James stay involved in the chapel program was a winner. And, the two church-trained volunteers were clearly sent by God to help in the work of the ministry. These partnerships provided a continuity that we were able to build on, and a unity that paved the way for the presence of God and the power of God to be experienced in ways we couldn't have imagined.

CHAPTER 3

Going Blind

My first Sunday at the FOB was Palm Sunday, one week before Easter. Eight people showed up for church that morning: Pastor James, four American soldiers who had been meeting with him faithfully for the past year, my Chaplain Assistant, one new guy, and me. It was easy to see that the soldiers respected James. He had been there for them, and they loved him. My sermon was based on Mark chapter eleven, "Blessed is he who comes in the name of the Lord." We finished worship having communion together, Pastor James and me side-by-side.

After I thanked everyone for coming and was about to dismiss the small group, a stranger in a Ukrainian army uniform walked into the chapel unannounced and proclaimed, "I have something to say."

He had an excellent command of English vocabulary, but with a heavy accent. He was an attractive, friendly man, about 6' 2" with short hair, heavy eyebrows, and green eyes.

"I am not a Christian. Several months ago, I started having problems with my eyes. I went to the doctors here in our medical clinic. They told me I had an incurable eye condition. They brought in a specialist who confirmed the diagnosis. He said there was nothing they could do for me. No treatment. No medicine. No surgery. He said my eyes would gradually get worse until I was totally blind. Last Sunday I came here and asked the men if they would pray for me." He pointed to James and said, "That man put his hands on my head and prayed. These other guys put their hands on me and prayed too."

I glanced at Pastor James, who nodded affirmatively.

"The next day, last Monday, I could see better, so I went back to the clinic. The doctors did the same tests all over again. This time, they said I don't have that disease. I have been back to the clinic to see the doctors almost every day this week. Your God healed me. I am not going to lose my eyes. I am so happy. How can I become a Christian?"

You could hear the sounds of surprise and amazement from the small congregation, especially from Pastor James and the men who had prayed with him the previous Sunday. In simple terms, I explained who Jesus was and what it meant to receive him as Lord and Savior.

I wasn't a part of the miracle of healing that he experienced the previous week. Pastor James and the others had prayed for him. But on my first Sunday at Camp Echo, I had the privilege of praying with this man, a captain in the Ukrainian army, as he asked Jesus to come into his heart. The feeling among our little group was incredible.

The Ukrainian brother came alive. Every time I saw him, whether walking down the street, sitting in the DFAC, or attending a staff meeting, he hugged me, told me how thankful he was that Jesus healed him and saved him. And then he'd say, "We have to tell people about Jesus. They have to know him."

He stayed two more months before his rotation ended. He attended worship every Sunday and Bible study every Tuesday night. Then his unit of about a hundred soldiers returned to the Ukraine. One last hug. One last expression of gratitude. One last "We have to tell people about Jesus. They have to know him." Then he was gone.

I haven't had any contact with him since he left, but I wonder where he is. I wonder if he's telling people about Jesus, if he's telling his friends and family and neighbors about the deteriorating eye disease, and how a group of five Americans, one black pastor and four white soldiers, prayed for him. I wonder if he still has the sense of urgency to tell people about the God who healed him.

That first Sunday set the tone for my time in Iraq. Word began to spread that exciting things were happening, and each week more people started worshipping with us. By the second month there were about forty-four on Sunday mornings, and by the third month, more than fifty. In addition to the Tuesday night Bible study, there were small groups meeting in various places on Wednesday, Thursday, and Friday. Some met at night, and some during the day to accommodate those who worked nights.

I led one of the groups, Pastor James led one, and the Lord brought us a few other mature Christians who provided leadership in the small groups and our chapel program. The war was still happening outside the wire, but inside the wire, something special was happening in the spiritual realm.

CHAPTER 4

I Wish I Were Catholic

There were no explosions on Easter Sunday morning. Certainly, the residents of Diwaniyah knew what day it was. Did they take the day off? Did they forget? Were they being kind to us, respecting that this was a special day for most Christians? Or were the attacks just going to come later in the day? Whatever the case, I was thankful for the peaceful morning. I got dressed and headed over to the chapel.

Celebrating Christ's resurrection is one of the high points of the year for many Christians, and to start the day without mortars made it even better. The sun was shining, but it wasn't hot yet. We enjoyed the music, and there were more than fifty in attendance. Pastor James prayed, read the scripture, and encouraged the people. I preached on the love of God, who gives opportunities for fresh starts. At the end of the message, I asked everyone to repeat a prayer of commitment to the Lord. Two people confessed faith in Christ for the first time, and it was an awesome celebration of the Resurrection.

The joy and camaraderie continued as we transitioned from worship to fellowship, with twenty-seven of us going over to the DFAC to have lunch together. The DFAC staff had decided to make Easter Sunday a special event, so the entire dining area was decorated in Easter colors and themes: banners, a huge Easter Bunny, streamers, and a special holiday menu. The food was always good, with a lot of options. But today we could select whatever our family's traditional Easter feast was back home: ham, turkey, roast beef, pumpkin pie. They also brought in a sound system and played music all afternoon. We enjoyed the festive sights, sounds, and tastes.

Even though there was a war going on, most supervisors had told their people that unless something came up, they could have the day off. Because of that, a lot of people lingered at the DFAC. We were far from home, lonely, and these people were our new family. Plus, the food was great. The joke among the soldiers was that everyone who came to Iraq joined *the 300 Club*. You either worked out every day at the MWR and got to the point where you could bench-press 300 pounds, or you spent a lot of time eating in the DFAC and ended up weighing 300 pounds.

I have to admit many of us ate way too much. I love desserts, and on Easter I focused my efforts on apple pie a la mode and pecan pie, also a la mode. And then, a few too many oatmeal raisin cookies. It was just a wonderful day: worship, celebrating the Risen Lord, fellowship with good brothers and sisters in Christ, great weather, and really good food.

After the last of our group left, I decided to go back to the office. The senior chaplain at Camp Victory required each chaplain to send a weekly report. That way he knew what was happening throughout the country. In the report, we commented on how things were going, the attendance at all our events, the number of counseling appointments, any casualties, unusual experiences, and whether we needed any equipment or supplies. Standard reporting in the military. I sent it in each week as requested.

After sending the official report, I would usually write a private email to my supervisor because he and I had a similar church background and I thought he would appreciate what was happening. People were coming to faith in Christ. Prayers were being answered. Exciting stuff was happening in the spiritual realm. I wanted to share with him details that were not appropriate to put into the official report, but were amazing nonetheless, so he could rejoice with me.

As I was writing the email around two-thirty in the afternoon, I heard the sirens, so I put on my Kevlar vest and helmet and ran down the hall to go out to the bunker, as shrapnel and gravel pelted the roof of the one-story building. The three explosions were really close. The first landed just to the left of my building, the second right outside, behind my office, and the third in the parking lot about a block away.

I ducked into the bunker outside the door, the Colonel and Sergeant Major soon joining me. Just three of us this time. On a typical day there might be more than a dozen of us crammed in there. After about five or six minutes, we heard the all-clear signal.

"Sir, it's been fun chatting with you, but if you'll excuse me, I have to run over to the clinic to see if we have any casualties."

"OK, Chaps. Let me know."

"Yes, sir. I will."

The medical clinic was a buzz of activity when I rushed in the front door. About twenty-five people crammed into a lobby that had only a dozen chairs. Six on one side facing the six on the other side. Not your typical waiting room, this area was mostly a place to drop your gear before going in to see a doc or nurse, or before going in to visit a patient.

"How many?" I asked SGT Robinson, the guy behind the counter.

"Four so far, Chaplain. No deaths reported as far as I know."

"Thanks."

A big part of a chaplain's job during war operations is to care for the wounded, which meant I spent a lot of time at the clinic. I knew all of the doctors, nurses, medics, and staff. I was there at least twice a day to check on them and their patients, and whenever there were casualties, they knew I would be there soon.

"May I go in?" I asked.

"Let me check." As he went through the swinging white doors, I could see several wounded soldiers being cared for by the medical staff. He came back into the waiting area. "Sure, Chaplain. Go on in."

Usually, when they were working on a patient, they'd take him or her into one of the smaller rooms for privacy, but today all four patients were in the large open area just inside the swinging doors. Two male nurses were extracting shrapnel from the legs, butt, and back of a female soldier. It was impossible to keep her covered while working on her. A doctor was examining a male soldier who seemed worse off than the female. His internal injuries would require surgery in Germany, and possibly a flight back to the United States.

The other two had less serious wounds. I went over to talk with them. When I asked one soldier how he was doing, he began to mutter, and there were tears in his eyes. I couldn't understand what he was saying, and assumed he was crying because of the pain. He mumbled something again. Then I understood his words and his tears. "I'm hurt, but my best friend is dead."

"Who?"

"My friend, Kelly."

"Your friend is dead?" I needed to clarify, because nobody had mentioned this to me.

"Yes. He was standing right next to me. The mortar landed on the other side of him, cutting him in half instantly. My injuries are nothing compared to what happened to him. He saved my life." It's difficult to imagine the conglomeration of thoughts and emotions going on inside this soldier.

I rushed out to see the receptionist. "Have you guys heard anything about someone being killed in that mortar attack?"

"No, not yet."

Just then, a Sergeant Major ran in. I hadn't seen him before. "Chaplain, we need you to come with us. We have a dead soldier and we have to evacuate him immediately. Are you a Catholic priest?"

Others from the unit started pouring into the clinic. During the next half-hour, more than a hundred people asked the same question, "Are you Catholic? Are you a priest?"

Never in my life did it hurt so much to say I was not Catholic. I wanted so badly to say, "Yes, I am a priest."

Sergeant Kelly was the most popular guy in the unit that had come down to Camp Echo for Operation Black Eagle. We needed the additional firepower, and many considered these visitors to be our rescuers—our heroes. For two weeks they fought al-Sadr's forces for control of Diwaniyah. In addition, U.S. and Coalition warplanes targeted insurgent positions with *Hellfire* missiles in and near the city.

Officials verified that six insurgents were killed and 39 captured. The detainees were housed in the building right next to my office, and sometimes I watched as they were trucked in and taken into the detention center, hoods on their heads, hands tied behind their backs. Although we weren't supposed to take pictures of the detainees, several people in our camp did.

Now that the operation was drawing to a close, the visiting troops were assembling at their vehicles to drive to their next location, when the three mortars landed.

Many of the people in the visiting unit were Catholic, including SGT Kelly. After the dust and smoke cleared, everyone in the unit saw him lying on the ground. They were traumatized. Kelly was, in a way, their emotional and spiritual leader—a devout, godly, personable man who cared deeply about each of them.

A recent college graduate, he could have entered the Army as an officer, but he wanted to experience life as an enlisted person before becoming an officer, so he enlisted instead. He was smart, friendly, had a great sense of humor, and was devoted to God and his church. His fellow soldiers loved and respected him. Now they needed a Roman Catholic Priest.

There was a Catholic chaplain at the FOB, a parish priest from Poland who served with the Coalition command element. His name was Father Wladislaw Jasica, pronounced as *Vlodislov Yasheetsa*. Most of us shortened the name, and referred to him as Father Wlad.

I met him in a bunker. Father Wlad was six foot two, with thick, black hair that never saw a comb, brown eyes, and a scruffy goatee. Before the war, he served in a parish in southern Poland, but had volunteered to minister in the Polish army as a Reservist. He was a Captain when with his soldiers at home, but wore the higher rank of Lieutenant Colonel when deployed. I was a Major, which is just between Captain and Lieutenant Colonel, so he outranked me and was the lead chaplain at the FOB. Fortunately, he spoke English well enough to converse, and to conduct mass for our troops. I spoke zero Polish.

After the Easter mortars exploded, Father Wlad was on the other side of the FOB attending to other casualties, and the chopper was waiting to take the remains of this soldier right now.

I conducted a flight-line memorial service as the helicopter crew prepared to take off. The men and women of the unit formed a double line extending from the medical clinic to the evac helicopter, wide enough for the funeral procession to march between the saluting soldiers. It was a tragic, but impressive sight. As the Blackhawk rotors thundered overhead, making it almost impossible to hear, I prayed for SGT Kelly and committed his soul to God. A Catholic chaplain would have to administer Last Rites somewhere else along the way.

After the chopper flew away, I stayed to talk and pray with many of the grieving, distraught soldiers. I hugged them and encouraged them as they told stories, anecdotes, and examples of the things SGT Kelly said or did. Like the way he befriended each of them regardless of rank. Or how he went out of his way to encourage and help them. Or a practical joke that always seemed to inspire them, not humiliate them.

It was gut-wrenching to be with them. They cried, and I cried with them. I went back into the clinic to talk and pray with those who were wounded. Then I returned to my office to amend my weekly report to Baghdad.

Late that night I had a phone appointment with my wife. She had flown from Atlanta to Southern California to attend a family reunion, and we had coordinated the times so I would be able to call while my parents, brothers and sisters, and extended family would all be together for Easter supper at my sister's house. The time difference was 11 hours, so to call while my family was gathered at 2 p.m. in California, I had to stay up to 1:00 in the morning.

Linda answered the phone and we talked for a while, but before I had a chance to tell her what had happened, she started passing the phone around to other family members who wanted to talk. "Don't do that," I yelled into the phone.

Emotionally, I wasn't ready to talk with anyone. What had started out as a fantastic Easter morning, turned into tragedy in the afternoon, but none of my family knew that.

In my discouragement, I didn't want to hear the sounds of laughter, forks and knives clinking against the plates, or the normal, happy conversation around the family table on a holiday. I didn't want to engage in casual, meaningless chitchat on the phone with my brothers and sisters. I was devastated, and they were jubilant.

I wanted to tell my wife, "Don't pass the phone around! I just want to talk with you!" but she had already taken the phone away from her ear, and couldn't hear me as she handed the phone to someone else. I screamed into the phone, hoping that she'd hear me, but it was too noisy at my sister's house. I screamed again, but nobody was listening. I was powerless, and hung up the phone.

Slowly, I walked to my hooch, the events of the day replaying in my mind. I was thrilled because of the two soldiers who gave their hearts to the Lord that morning, but pretty shaken by the casualties later on in the day. I was so tired I decided not to set the alarm clock, and slept more than twelve hours.

For all Christians, Catholic and Protestant, the Resurrection of Jesus Christ is a celebration of life over death, healing after hurting, and overcoming suffering. I had experienced all of it in one day, the good and the bad, and had no idea what the next day or two would bring. I fell into a depression, or an emotional slump, that lasted three days. It might have gone on longer, but I was too busy.

A lot of good was happening, mixed in with the many painful aspects of being away from home and at war. I read my Bible every day, and took time each afternoon to listen to Christian music and pray. I worked out in the mornings, and stayed in touch with other believers, gathering with them as often as possible. After a few days, the joy of the Lord returned stronger than ever.

CHAPTER 5

A Soul A Week, That's All We Ask

In 1986, Blue Diamond Growers in California initiated an ad campaign asking shoppers to buy a can of almonds each week. This was based on the fact that one almond tree produces fifty-two cans of almonds per year, and there are exactly fifty-two weeks in a year. Their slogan? "A can a week, that's all we ask." You can still find the old commercials on YouTube.

When I told my wife during a phone call that someone at Camp Echo was coming to faith in Christ every week, she recalled the TV commercial from years earlier and said, "A soul a week, that's all we ask." Being from California, I understood the allusion right away.

Linda had been praying that every week, someone would come to faith in Christ, and it was happening: someone at church on Sunday, a visitor to my office during the week, or a soldier in a unit training area. She prayed for the people I was ministering to, and God answered her prayers: a soul a week.

When I was a rookie chaplain, my supervisor showed up one day to mentor me. "Here's my philosophy of serving as a military chaplain: ministry follows friendship. If you love your soldiers and spend time with them and they know you like them, then they'll come to you when they want to talk about their spiritual need. Just love them, spend time with them, and trust the Holy Spirit to draw them. When they are ready to talk about the Lord, they'll know who to go to."

That sounded pretty good to me, so I adopted his philosophy of chaplain ministry. It was an effective approach throughout my military career, and it was true in Iraq. Here are some of the people I encountered as the Lord was reaching out to them by his Spirit.

LAUGHIN' AND PRAYIN'

One Tuesday morning a big ol' boy stepped into my office, and entered the Kingdom of God. He walked in unannounced. "Mind if I drop my body armor, chaplain?" It was already hitting the floor before I had a chance to reply.

"Not at all. Be my guest. Where are you from?"

"I'm from Brevard, North Carolina."

"Brevard? I've been to Brevard."

"Pity you," he laughed loud at his own joke. "What were you doin' in my town?"

"A friend of mine lives there. I was passing through and stopped to visit for a couple hours. Now, what are you doin' in my office?"

"I grew up in church, but never got serious 'bout Jesus or nuthin.' Just out o' boot camp an' AIT, an' they send me here. So, I figure if I'm gonna die right here in the desert at the ripe ol' age of 19, might as well get saved, confess my sins, whole nine yards, make things right, ya know."

I don't think I've ever had as much fun praying with someone as I did with him that day. Six feet four, a muscular 225-pounder with short brown hair and medium brown eyes. He walked loud, talked loud, and lived loud. I imagine he even sinned loud.

"Hey! I even know what to pray," he grinned.

"OK, you go first, then I'll pray."

"Gotcha!"

He was right; he knew what to do, and he prayed a great prayer. I don't recall ever hearing someone telling God jokes during a confessional prayer, but he did. We both started laughing. He kept on praying right through our laughter.

"Hey! I bet even the Lord has a sense of humor. Not a problem laughin' during prayer, is it, Chaplain?"

"Not a problem. I'm sure God is laughing too. Along with all his angels up there!"

"Ha!" Then he started naming his sins from childhood, high school, basic training, all the way up to a couple days ago. Sins with girls, booze, cigarettes, lyin', stealin', cheatin' in school, missin' church. Then he concluded with, "An' I ain't sinned the past coupla days, Lord, so I guess that brings me up to date. Come into my heart. Amen!" Just like that, he was done.

When he finished praying, I was laughing so hard, I don't think I could have prayed yet, so I suggested that we talk for a while and get acquainted before I take my turn.

A few days before this encounter, he was wearing his body armor while working, and injured his spine. It looked like the Army was getting ready to send him back to Brevard because he was in non-stop pain.

"So, I guess, I'm going home unless Jesus heals me."

"Well, let's pray about that too," I suggested.

"Gotcha! Your turn to pray."

Besides talking to the Lord about the young man's back injury, my prayer was that his commitment to Christ would be genuine and lifelong, regardless of whether he stayed in the Army or went home, whether the Lord healed his back or not.

When I finished praying, my new friend looked at me, grinned and said, "Shoot, when I get home an' show up at church, my pastor's gonna have a heart attack. I don't think he ever thought I was gonna get saved. Boy will he be surprised."

He looked at his watch. "Whoa! Gotta get back to work. Hey! By the way. Can I get a Bible? When's church?"

I handed him a Bible. "Church is at ten hundred Sunday, nineteen hundred Tuesday, and any time, any day you manage to find me."

"Great. I'll be your usher and deacon. You can count on it." He hefted his body armor and Kevlar, grimaced with pain, and left just as loudly as he came. Just like that, he was gone.

The young man started coming to church. As promised, he got there early to help set up chairs and serve as usher, greeter, deacon, bulletin-passer-outer, altar worker, whatever I asked him to do. He was a tremendous addition to the ministry team. He stayed afterwards to help clean up. Then went to the DFAC with a group of us for lunch. It took about a month for him to process out and return to North Carolina. I wish I could have seen the look on his pastor's face when he walked in the door of that Baptist church in Brevard.

SCRIPTURE WITH A TEXAS TWANG

One day, right after morning explosions, I decided to do an inside workout at the MWR, which stands for *Morale, Welfare, and Recreation*, instead of outside at the track. I usually visited with the MWR staff before getting on a treadmill, to see how they were doing. This morning, one of the personal trainers asked to talk privately with me. Lori was 5'1" with sparkling blue eyes and long blond hair that she sometimes wore straight and sometimes in pigtails. She had a slight Texas twang when she spoke.

"Good Morning, Chaplain."

"Hi, Lori. How's it going?"

"Things are fine, but I think it's about time I started coming to church. It's been a while."

"That'd be great. I'd love to have you join us. Tell me a bit about yourself."

"Where do I start. Hmmm. Let's see. We're from Texas. My husband is a Highway Patrol officer, although he's trying to get a job here so we can be together. No Kids. We used to go to church a bit back home; not much. But I think the Lord is stirring something up inside me, and I need to respond."

She started coming on Sundays, and loved the music. One time I asked if she would read the Bible text before I preached. After that, she wanted to read every Sunday.

"How about if you do the reading every other week, alternating with the Captain"

An FBI agent back home, and a member of the Army Reserve, the Captain was one of the guys in the Hummer that blew up, and was pulled out through the turret by the gunner. A regular in worship when his team wasn't out on patrol, he liked reading the scriptures, too. He'd grown up in the church, his father was a pastor, so he was pretty familiar with how to lead a worship service. I have no doubt he could have done it all without me there, just like Pastor James and my two volunteer assistants. They were a talented and spiritual group.

After she'd been worshipping with us a few weeks, Lori saw me in the MWR one day and approached. "Hey, Chaplain. Nice to see you again. I have a question for you."

"What's your question?"

"You've done so much for me, helping me get on track with the Lord, and I'd like to do something for you."

"Oh yeah? What do you have in mind?"

"Would you let me design a fitness program for you? I mean, that's my specialty at my fitness center back home. And I'd like to do that as a way of thanking you."

"That would be awesome, Lori," I said. But privately, I wondered how much work she was going to put me through, how much torture her program would entail, what it might include. Plus, I knew I needed to lose some weight, but was it that obvious?

"Come back tomorrow, and I'll start working with you," she instructed.

When I went back to the gym the next morning, she was all set up. "You already do enough for cardio and upper body strength. What you need is to work on your abs." She demonstrated ten exercises she wanted me to do, some on the mat, and others on the bench. Told me how many reps and how many days a week to do each exercise. I did those faithfully the rest of the time I was at Camp Echo, and the program made a big difference for me. Lori helped quite a few of the men and women at the FOB. And she stayed active in worship–and reading the scriptures.

I'M GOING TO KILL 'EM

One afternoon, I got an emergency call. "Chaplain! Come quick! One of our soldiers is on top of a hooch with his weapon, threatening to shoot the people inside. The commander says if you can't talk him down, he'll order someone to shoot him." I ran over to the housing area, and sure enough, he was up there with his M-16, screaming, cussing, and crying. I asked someone his name, and who was inside. Did anyone know what led up to this situation? The guy was an E-4 who worked in the motor pool. Nobody knew who was inside the hooch.

"Specialist, what are you doing?" I asked.

"I'm going to kill 'em both," he cried.

"Who's in there? And why do you want to kill them?"

"I'm going to kill 'em both," he repeated.

"Who? And Why?"

He looked at me. "Chaplain, my best friend's in there with my girlfriend. And I'm going to kill 'em both." This is not a direct quote. The graphic language he actually used would make this an R-rated story.

"Look, if you do that, your pain won't be any better. The only way to make this situation better is to put down your rifle, come down, and go with me to my office where we can talk."

I didn't know whether he could see the snipers the commander had positioned nearby, waiting for the signal to shoot. I didn't know if he was going to pull the trigger and kill his friend and his girlfriend. I didn't know if my being there would make any difference to this young man who had been betrayed by the people he was closest to. I didn't know if he was going to turn the gun on himself. Some people in his circumstances opt for suicide because the pain is so great.

"Let's make a deal. It's hot out here. If you come down and talk with me, we'll go to my office, get a Coke, and talk. Just you and me. We'll spend the day together and sort things out. Then you can decide what you want to do."

The thermometer on the wall of the HQ building pointed to 120 degrees, but that was as high as the numbers went. The needle was pressed up against the little pin by the 120, which meant it was probably more than 120 in the shade that day. The angry, distraught soldier was on top of a metal *containerized housing unit*, basically a steel storage crate. It had to be hotter up there than down here.

"Listen to me? If you shoot them, you're going to ruin three lives–theirs, and yours."

Slowly, he put the gun down on the roof, lowered his head and sobbed. Then he climbed down, leaving the M-16 on top of the hooch. Several MPs apprehended him as I went to the Colonel.

"Sir, I told him I would take him to my office for a Coke and talk things through. I am requesting that you let me do that before you take him into custody." The commander had the authority to do whatever he wanted to do. I had no authority. He could say yes or no.

"How much time you think you'll need, Chaps?"

"I don't know. Depends on whether he wants to talk. Could be 15 minutes, could be a few hours."

The Colonel was in a tough spot and wasn't sure what to do, so I continued. "Sir, he doesn't have a weapon. It's still up there on the hooch. And there are no weapons in my office, so he can't do any harm. Give me two hours? You can post the MPs either just outside the building, or just inside where it's air conditioned. There's no way he can escape. After two hours, he's yours. What do you say?"

"OK, Chaplain," was all the Colonel said to me. He ordered the MPs to escort the soldier to my office and stand watch in the hall just outside my door. He directed another guy to retrieve the weapon from the roof.

In the office, I saw the guy up close for the first time. Like the good ol' boy from Brevard, he was only 19. He finished high school a year ago and enlisted in the Army three days later. Five foot ten, 160 pounds, sandy brown, wispy hair, and a sadness in his eyes that seemed to predate the events of this day. He'd been at the FOB about six months, met a young female soldier in the DFAC one night, and was smitten. After a few days, she moved into his hooch. She was his first love.

"What happened today?" I asked the young man.

"When I got to Camp Echo, I was a nobody. I never had a girlfriend. When I met her, I was a virgin. She changed my life. I thought it was true love. We talked about getting married as soon as we got back from Iraq. We liked the same music. Same movies. Man, I've never had that feeling before. That feeling like, like, like, like I was special to someone. Like my life mattered. For the first time ever, I was happy.

"Last night I worked the night shift, and when I got back to the hooch this morning, the door was locked. I knocked on the door, but she didn't answer. I put my ear to the door, and heard them inside. I banged on the door, but they wouldn't open it. That's when I climbed onto the roof. There's a small hole right over my bed. Lying on my bed, I can see the sunlight. When I got up there and peeked into that hole, I saw them naked on the bed.

"I thought she loved me. I thought we were going to be together for the rest of our lives. I thought he was my friend. He was my friend."

"Why didn't you pull the trigger?"

"I don't know. I wanted to and I didn't want to. Is it possible to love and hate someone at the same time?"

"I'm not sure how to answer that one. I don't know if there is an answer. That's what life throws at us sometimes, though. So yeah, I think it is possible."

"How could she tell me she loves me one night, and then do this the next morning?"

"That's a tough one, too. What do you think?

"I don't know. I feel like she's been using me. I feel like a fool. I thought she loved me. And I don't know which is worse – to be betrayed by her or by the guy I thought was my best friend. I trusted him. I trusted him with my very life. And then he does this to me?"

We sat in silence for a few minutes. I prayed silently while he agonized, squirmed, cried. He pounded his fist onto his thigh— six, seven, eight times. Then for the first time, looked me in the eye, and out of the blue asked, "Is there a God?"

I was startled. I pray for my soldiers every day. Still I wondered, *Where did that come from?*

"Yes, my friend. I'm pretty sure there is a God. But not everyone thinks there is."

"I grew up in a family that was pretty messed up. We don't believe in God. I've never even been to church. If there is a God, can he help me?"

"Yes, he can. But the kind of help God will give you might not keep you in the Army. Might not keep you out of jail. You're still in trouble after what happened out there. But what God can do is help you take care of what's happening inside you as a person, in your mind, your emotions, your attitudes, your spirit. He can change what's happening on the inside, and when that is healthy, then he'll help you take care of things on the outside–things like relationships, decisions, and behavior. These things flow from what's going on in the inner man. And it's the inner man where God can make a huge difference for any of us."

He never heard anything like this before, and he had a funny look on his face. "If it's true, and God can do that for me, what do I have to do to be—what do you call it—saved?"

"There's a story in the Bible about a guy who asked that exact question to another guy named Paul. Let me read it to you." I read him Acts 16:25-34.

||||||||||||||||||||||||||||||||||||||||||||||||||||||||||||||||||||||||||||||||||||||||||||||||||||||||||||||||||||||||||||

About midnight Paul and Silas were praying and singing hymns to God, and the prisoners were listening to them. Suddenly there was such a violent earthquake that the foundations of the jail were shaken, and immediately all the doors were opened, and everyone's chains came loose. When the jailer woke up and saw the doors of the prison open, he drew his sword and was going to kill himself, since he thought the prisoners had escaped.

But Paul called out in a loud voice, "Don't harm yourself, because all of us are here!" Then the jailer called for lights, rushed in, and fell down trembling before Paul and Silas. Then he escorted them out and said, "Sirs, what must I do to be saved?" So, they said, "Believe on the Lord Jesus, and you will be saved—you and your household." Then they spoke the message of the Lord to him along with everyone in his house. He took them the same hour of the night and washed their wounds. Right away he and all his family were baptized. He brought them into his house, set a meal before them, and rejoiced because he had believed God with his entire household.

||||||||||||||||||||||||||||||||||||||||||||||||||||||||||||||||||||||||||||||||||||||||||||||||||||||||||||||||||||||||||||

"I don't know very much about God and the Bible, but I guess I gotta start somewhere. Will you pray with me and help me?"

"Yes, I will."

When we finished praying, he stood up and said, "Well, I guess it's time to face the music. Pray for me and wish me luck." He shook my hand, thanked me, and opened the door to the waiting MPs.

Chapter 6

Eye-in-the-Sky

The year before I went to Iraq, my son Kevin was there as an infantry officer. Most of the guys in his battalion had no respect for their chaplain because he refused to go "outside the wire" when the soldiers went out on patrol. Instead, the chaplain chose the safety of staying at the FOB. After returning to the States, Kevin told me, "Dad, I'm a Christian, and I wouldn't go to that chaplain's worship services. I had no respect for him. When *you* go to Iraq, make sure *you* go wherever your soldiers have to go. They'll love you for it."

Hearing that from Kevin confirmed what I had known and practiced as a pastor and then as a chaplain. People respond to you personally and spiritually when you spend time with them in their setting, or in a context where they don't feel at a disadvantage. When I was pastoring in Southern California, I used to visit the workplaces of the people in the church. Most of them loved it. During the summers, we had a church campout near a lake. We went to ball games together.

Spending time with people where they liked to hang out *balanced the ledger* in the relationship. The church is where the pastor is comfortable, and many non-clergy are less comfortable, feeling they are at a disadvantage. On the other hand, where they work and play and eat is where they have an edge, so it evens the playing field. This practice resulted in natural opportunities to talk, to get to know each other, and open up.

When I found out that the Military Transition Team I was assigned to went outside the wire to patrol the nearby city of Diwaniyah, I was determined to go with them, despite the dangers. A Military Transition Team, often referred to as a MiTT, is a 10–15-man team that trains local forces. The MiTTs in Iraq trained, mentored, and advised the Iraqi Security Forces in all aspects of warfighting operations and tactics. The goal was to help the Iraqi forces become capable of conducting counterinsurgency operations without our assistance.

My team had twelve men, nice guys, but their training and experiences had hardened them, turning them into tough, mission-focused fighters. Most had no interest in religion. They would train and mentor the Iraqi Army (IA), and at the end of the day, sleep in their Hummers on a bridge outside Diwaniyah so they could keep an eye on the city and be close enough to respond quickly if they were needed. Sometimes they slept on the ground at IA headquarters, returning to Camp Echo every third or fourth day to sleep, refuel, eat some real food, and take a shower.

They were quite surprised when I told them I wanted to go out on patrol with them, because rumor had it that chaplains weren't allowed to go outside the wire, leaving the safety of the FOB, or that chaplains were afraid to go. I had heard the same rumors, and had checked with the MNC-I chaplain, up at Camp Victory near Baghdad, to see if it was true. He told me there were no restrictions; I could go with the MiTT if I felt like it, and if they'd let me.

When I told the team I wanted to go out on patrol with them, they were surprised. "What? You want to go out and do what we do?" some of the guys yelled to me, laughing incredulously.

"Well, not exactly," I answered. "I can't do what you do, but I want to be with you, go where you go, experience the same situations you deal with, and see life through your eyes."

"We never heard of a chaplain who wanted to go out where the real stuff happened. Sure. Get your gear and go with us tomorrow. We leave at 1700."

My son was right. The moment I told my team I wanted to go out with them, our relationship changed. They respected me, trusted me, and felt they could talk with me about personal matters. That was the day I became their chaplain.

At 1700 (5:00 p.m.) the next day, we got in the Hummers and drove four miles to the IA compound to meet with the Iraqi leadership. Thirteen of us in four Hummers. After discussing the plans for the next two days, the Iraqi General invited our team inside for dinner. What a feast. It was my first time eating Iraqi food. The General was a gracious host: friendly, generous, and kind. His wife made a brief appearance, and then disappeared. We didn't see his six children, who were teens and young adults still living at home.

The General spoke to us through an interpreter. He talked of life during Saddam Hussein's reign–the fear, uncertainty, and terror. He described his hope for a better Iraq, a better economy, safer communities, and education. He was thankful the American and Coalition Forces were there to help rebuild his country. He told stories, laughed, and asked about our lives, our families, our hopes and dreams. After the meal, we returned to our trucks, rolled out our sleeping bags on the ground, but didn't get into them. It was too hot.

Waking at 0500 (5:00 a.m.), the MiTT commander, a Major, spent the first couple of hours of the day inside with the Iraqi leaders, going over the plan for a raid in Diwaniyah. The MiTT's job was to go into the city with the IA in order to catch some suspected terrorists, take possession of their weapons, and then come home—routine operation for them, exciting and scary for me.

We drove to a busy residential part of the city. Dozens of high-rise apartment buildings encircled several soccer fields where hundreds of children were playing. Literally, thousands of people milled about as we got out of the trucks. The soldiers began searching homes for the terrorists, weapons, and ammunition. I didn't go into any of the buildings. Instead, I stayed with a couple of guys who had to keep an eye on the vehicles. Standing outside the Hummers, we talked as we scanned the crowd. We had to stay alert because anyone in the pressing crowd might have a gun or a knife. Anyone might be wearing an explosive device underneath his or her clothing, and a lot of people came up close to talk to us or see us. Many of them spoke English. Several had visited the United States.

"I've been to Disney World," one man mentioned. Another asked, "Where do you live?" After I told him, he said, "I've been there!" A few thanked us for helping to stabilize their country. Of course, there were some who wanted us to leave and never come back. The children played soccer the entire time.

After an hour searching for men and weapons, the team came up empty-handed. One resident told the Major that several people saw us coming and warned the terrorists. They got away just as we arrived. So, we got back into the trucks, the crowd still pressing. Several children tried to get into the Hummer. A few teens invited us to play soccer.

When the doors were closed and locked and the engines running, the MiTT commander got on the radio to give instructions.

"We'll drive straight ahead four blocks. At the stop sign, take a left, drive a quarter of a mile and turn right, taking that road back to the IA compound. Any questions?"

There were no questions. The radio operator in each truck responded with an affirmative. Then, just after we started moving, a different voice came on the net. I didn't get the guy's name, but I got his message loud and clear.

"Do not turn left at that intersection. *Eye-in-the-Sky* detected a hot spot. Do not turn left at that stop sign. Again, do not turn left."

After a brief silence, the Major came back on the radio. "OK . . . Let's turn right at the intersection, and take the alternate route. Turn right at the stop sign."

"Roger."

Eye-in-the-Sky is what we called a drone with a camera, but it also had the ability to detect heat. There's no way of knowing what a "hot spot" might be. It could be a dog, a rabbit, a person, or an IED. The *Eye-in-the-Sky* just knows something is there, so we have to be careful. We requested one for this operation, but we didn't always get what we asked for, so we didn't know for sure that it'd be up there this time. Apparently, it was.

Our convoy approached the intersection, came to a stop, and turned right. Less than ten seconds after we made the turn, a huge explosion occurred exactly where we would have been had we turned left as planned. The guys in our Hummer stared at each other incredulously. We all understood. Had the drone not been up there, this could have been our day to die. Instead, as the 2002 James Bond film was titled, we would live to *Die Another Day*.

Aside from the fear of dying, I had an unrelenting fear that I would lose my leg in Iraq. I realized that if the *Eye-in-the-Sky* hadn't warned us, we would have turned left at the intersection, and our worst fears might have been realized.

Then I remembered a friend of mine, John, who works at Northrop-Grumman. His department makes the gyroscopes that guide the drones used by our military. I made a mental note to call him when I got a chance, to thank him for saving my life.

John Reno is a big man. Six foot three, two hundred fifty pounds, sixty-something years of age, with graying hair that looks good in a rugged sort of way. A full mustache that could easily be a handlebar if he wanted it to be, but isn't quite. Yet, for all his impressive, dominant appearance, John is gentle in voice and spirit. A brilliant engineer, planner, and administrator, he heads up the team that produces Northrop-Grumman's most popular, most effective gyroscope.

I met John and his family in 2001 when I moved to West Valley City, Utah. They had met my dad years before and had become friends. When my dad told them he had a son who was coming to the Salt Lake Valley, John called me sight unseen and offered to let my family live with them until we had a place of our own. We went to church with them. Our son went to school with their daughter. Our dogs played together. To this day, I consider John one of my very best friends.

Two days after the *Eye-in-the-Sky* warned us about the hot spot, I called him from Iraq. After catching up on what was going on in our lives, I told him what happened, and finished with, "John, I want to thank you for saving my life."

"Well, I'll be! I have been praying for you every day. And I knew the military was using my gyroscope. But never in my wildest imagination did I think it would save the life of my friend."

CHAPTER 7

Interpreter's Dream

While I was in Iraq, I read a daily devotional from Henry and Richard Blackaby titled *Experiencing God Day-By-Day*. After writing the classic book *Experiencing God*, they co-authored a new set of devotions, written in such a way that readers can experience God each day in new and fresh ways. Here is an excerpt from the May 8 reading.

> *It is possible for us to be so busy trying to bring God into our activity that we don't even notice Him at work around us. He seeks to redirect our attention so that we might join Him, but we tend to be self-centered, evaluating everything by how it affects us. We must learn to view events around us from God's perspective. Then we will see our world very differently. When God brings someone across our path . . . we will then*

adjust our lives to join God as He works in that person's life. We ought to live each day with tremendous anticipation as we look to see where God is working around us. As our eyes are opened to His activity, we will marvel at His great works (Experiencing God Day-By-Day, B&H Publishers, p.129).

After reading this in the morning, I prayed that the Lord would open my eyes to what he was already doing, and that he would invite me to join in his activity. This concept was in my mind all day with a sense of anticipation. But all day long, everything was rather routine. There was nothing spectacular . . . until I went to the DFAC for dinner.

After going through the line to get my food, I found a place to sit, and noticed that many of the guys at the table were from a visiting unit. They were sent to Camp Echo to assist in searching the neighboring city for weapons and terrorists. They would be at our location only as long as it took to get the job done, which ended up being less than two weeks.

A young captain sitting directly across from me noticed that I was a chaplain and said, "Hey, Chaps! My terp needs to see you. But it has to be a secret."

During operations in the Middle East, coalition forces employ locals who speak English to serve as interpreters. We called them *terps*, which is a shortened form of *interpreters*.

"He doesn't want anyone to see him talking with you, especially the other terps."

Just then the interpreter arrived at the table and sat down next to the captain. As soon as he saw the cross on my uniform, he picked up his tray, scurried around the table, and took the seat next to mine. He leaned in close and asked, "Are you a Christian?"

"Yes."

on to make. Can we talk"?

...w 'bout after dinner?"

No. Tomorrow. Maybe afternoon?"

"Can you meet me at two o'clock?"

He looked at the captain, who nodded. "Yes. Where?"

I told him where my office was, and asked the captain if he could see that he got there.

"No problem, Chaps."

The question flashed into my mind, "Could this be the encounter I had been waiting for all day? The devotional reading that morning made a big impression on me, and I had been praying throughout the day. Could this be what the Lord and *the Blackabys* were preparing me for?

The next afternoon, the interpreter showed up right on time, and told me his name, which was not really his name. "We don't use our real names because it would not be safe if anyone found out we were working for the Americans. Call me Danny."

"Nice to meet you, Danny. Tell me about yourself."

"I learned to speak English from watching Hollywood movies."

I thought that was hilarious. "You learned English from the movies?"

"Yes. We watch a lot of movies, some of them many times, and I memorized the lines. Phonetically at first, but after many movies and several years, I began to understand. When the Americans started looking for interpreters, I took the test and scored well enough to get the job. I hope to work for your Army for two years, because after two years I can qualify to go to America. When I get there, I want to marry a Christian woman. I will not marry a

Muslim woman. But if this job doesn't last two years, then I
to stay here."

Danny was a little taller and thinner than I was, with dark,
short, curly hair, and deep, brown, pensive eyes. Twenty-six years
old and good-looking, he spoke English well with a noticeable
accent. He told me where he grew up and about his family,
making me promise never to tell anyone, explaining that it would
be dangerous for him if the people in his city were to find out what
he was doing.

"Why do you want to talk to me, Danny?"

He had been planning this conversation for more than a year,
not knowing who it would be with, but determined that he had to
find someone he could trust. Someone he could talk to about his
dream. Someone who could tell him about Jesus.

"The other terps will not be happy if they know I came to see
you. They don't want any of us to talk with Christians. But let me
tell you what happened to me."

I was sitting on the edge of my seat, waiting to hear his story.

"When I was a boy, my family would go from our city to
Baghdad to visit relatives. I would go outside and play with other
children in the neighborhood. One boy in particular became my
friend, and after a while he asked if I wanted to go inside for a
drink of water. It gets hot here in Iraq."

"Yes, I've noticed."

He continued. "When we went into his home for the water,
I noticed on the wall a picture of Jesus, a picture of Mary, and a
cross. We drank the water, then went out to play."

Danny spoke slowly at first, carefully choosing his words, but
he became more comfortable the longer we talked.

"Every year, we went back to Baghdad, and every year I played
with my friend. Every year we would go in for a drink of water.

Still on the wall, the pictures of Jesus, Mary, and the cross. And I noticed something . . . his family. They were happy.

"After the third year of seeing these things in my friend's house, my family and I were in the car on the way home and I asked my mother if I could have a picture of Jesus. She got angry and yelled at me. 'You will never have a picture of Jesus. We are not Christian. We are Muslim.' So, I knew I could not talk to my mother about Jesus.

"Now I am twenty-six. One year ago, just before I started working for your Army, I had a dream. In my dream, Jesus came to me, put his hand on my head like this, and talked to me. But I could not hear his words."

Danny leaned forward and looked deep into my eyes. "Can you tell me what Jesus said to me in my dream?"

Several things raced through my mind. I thought of the stories in the Bible, of Joseph and his dreams, and how he interpreted dreams for his family, and then for Pharaoh. I thought of Daniel, who explained dreams to Nebuchadnezzar. Apparently, God has been using dreams for thousands of years to speak to the people of the Middle East. Apparently, he still speaks in dreams.

I was convinced that this is what the Lord was preparing me for. I prayed yesterday in anticipation of an unknown encounter. I prayed today in preparation for this conversation with Danny. As soon as he asked the question, the Lord revealed to me what he said to Danny in that dream.

"Yes, I can tell you what Jesus said to you. Jesus told you that he loves you. He wants to be your friend. He forgives you for the terrible things you have done. He is the true God. And he wants you to live for him and worship him. He will forgive you, wash away your sin, and be close to you every single day, no matter what happens to you."

That's when Danny started to cry. "Would you help me pray?"

"Of course, I will."

Tears ran down both sides of his face as he repented of his sins and asked Jesus to come into his heart. After he finished praying, he opened his eyes, looked at me, and said, "When I am done working for your army, and go back to my hometown, my friends and my family will kill me. But at last I know Jesus. I love Jesus."

His comments took me by surprise. How could he know what his friends and family would do? I had to ask, "Have you killed someone who converted to Christianity?"

"Yes, I have killed several friends who left Islam. So, I know what they will do. But it's OK now. I know Jesus now. I love Jesus."

I've heard about people who've been tortured or killed because of their faith in Christ. But this was the first time I talked with someone who admitted to killing Christians. It reminded me of St. Paul in the New Testament. He, too, persecuted Christians, but then he experienced a dramatic conversion and became a powerful force for Christianity. Could Danny become a dynamic witness for Christ? There's no telling what he might do with his life and his newfound faith if he survived this war, and if he survived his friends and family.

I was amazed by his statement of love for Jesus, and realized that the Spirit of God had been speaking to Danny for more than eighteen years, leading up to last year's dream, and culminating in this encounter.

He spoke with strength and passion, and I was impressed by the clarity he had about counting the cost and living for the Lord. It was immediately clear that even though he knew the risks, he didn't intend to stay quiet about his new faith in Christ. He planned to tell his friends and family.

I also noticed the stark contrast in what it means for different people to "count the cost" of being a disciple of Jesus Christ. When American Christians let others know about their faith, the result might be ridicule, mockery, or people thinking less of them. In some cases, it might mean a ruined reputation or the loss of friends, and occasionally it leads to a divorce. Danny had already considered the cost, and for him, that price would be his life, and he knew it. I'll never forget his voice as he said, "At last I know Jesus. I love Jesus."

Our encounter lasted about three hours. Then Danny had to get back to his unit. They were going into town that night to finish their work, and would leave the next day. As we said goodbye, I told him I would continue praying for him. He held both of my hands tight, then hugged me for a long time. It was a hundred and some degrees that day. I noticed his perspiration, but that was of no consequence. What mattered was who he was as a human being and as a child of God. I told him I hoped to see him again.

But the story isn't finished yet.

It took me a few days to find out where Danny's unit went. They moved to a different city, miles away, to fight insurgents and capture weapons caches, the same reasons they had come to Diwaniyah and Camp Echo.

After several inquiries, I finally got the name of a chaplain at the new location and sent him an email. We didn't know each other, so the message was probably received with some degree of skepticism. I didn't even know if he was a Christian, and if so, what denomination he might be, so I had no idea what he believed about conversion, discipleship, and baptism. Still, I wrote about Danny and our conversation. Then, hoping I was following the leading of the Holy Spirit, I wrote in the email, "Your job is to find Danny, baptize him, and disciple him."

The next day I received a terse email from the other chaplain. "I don't know who you are. And I don't know who Danny is. But if he shows up here, I'll talk to him."

That was it. No warmth, no compassion, no "Praise God, isn't this wonderful." I wanted Danny to know there were others he could talk with, others he could trust, but this didn't sound very promising.

Two weeks went by without hearing anything from Danny or the other chaplain. Then one night, after a late visit to the medical clinic, I stopped by the office to put some things away before going to my hooch to get some sleep. There on my computer screen was an email from the other chaplain that read, "I just had to tell you I met Danny. You were right. His conversion is genuine. He comes to Bible study every day. Tonight I baptized him. I will disciple him as long as he's here at my FOB."

I was so excited I couldn't sleep. I wanted to call my wife right away and tell her about it, but because of the time difference, I had to wait until the next day. When I finally reached her, the first thing she said was, "You have to tell Kevin."

"Why do I need to tell Kevin?"

"He told me on the phone the other day that he prays for you every day, and prays specifically that you would lead a real Iraqi to the Lord."

I had been praying daily and fasting one day a week before and during the deployment. Because of my denomination's Church Connection Plan, there were four congregations back in the States praying regularly for me. I knew my wife prayed for me. And now, I found out that my son was praying specifically for an Iraqi to come to Christ. It's amazing to watch God in action, and to see how he leads his people to participate in what he's doing, even if only by praying. I was deeply moved, and grateful.

The Bible teaches us that some things will not happen without prayer and fasting. I am convinced that one of the reasons behind the supernatural experiences I witnessed while in Iraq was the tremendous prayer support that I had.

I'm also grateful for the guidance I received at exactly the right time from the devotional *Experiencing God Day-By-Day*. Dr. Blackaby was right. God had been working in Danny's life long before I got to Camp Echo. I just needed to ask God to show me what he was already doing, and then prayerfully prepare to join in His activity.

I often wonder about Danny. I wonder what his real name is. I wonder if he's alive, if he ever made it to the United States, and if he ever married a Christian woman. I wonder if he told the story of his dream and conversion to his friends and family, and if so, how did they respond? I wonder how many others dreamed about the Lord, and if so, who was there to tell them about Jesus and his love.

CHAPTER 8

Shaking with Fear

The daily attacks continued. People were getting hurt, and I was in the medical clinic two or three times a day. I conducted memorial services and ceremonies every week.

Right after Sunday morning worship one day, two soldiers came up to me while I was still inside the chapel. One was a Lieutenant Colonel named Steve, commander of a Border Transition Team (BiTT), who had become a good friend to me. The other was a Sergeant First Class, a medic on the same BiTT. Everyone called him *Doc*. He was between 35–40 years old, a guitarist and a worship leader back at his home church. He often led worship during Bible studies and small group sessions at Camp Echo. The other men were regular participants in worship, so I knew them pretty well.

"Hi, guys. What's up?"

Doc spoke first. "Chaplain, we were out on patrol last Wednesday when our Hummer ran over an IED. Instantly the truck burst into flames, with all of us on fire and trapped inside. All four of the doors jammed so we couldn't open them. The only way out was through the hatch, so the gunner up top pulled us out one by one, and put out the fire on every one of us. Saved our lives. Thanks to him, we all made it out alive, even though we all got some burns."

"Oh, wow!" I exclaimed. "I'm glad you guys are alive."

"Yeah. For a while there, it didn't look like we were going to make it."

I could see burns on both of his hands and on one side of his neck. "So, what's on your mind now, Doc?"

"Chaplain, ever since that experience, my hands started shaking, and I can't stop. I thought it'd go away after a day, maybe two. But it doesn't stop. I can't sleep, they shake so much. The doc says it's stress or fear. Maybe a combination. I don't think I'm afraid, but I guess I am. And I don't feel like I'm stressing, but I can't stop the shakes. The problem is that I can't do my job, and my boss says he's gonna send me home. But I don't wanna leave when the rest of my guys are staying here. I wanna stay and complete the mission, finish the job we came here to do, and go home together as a team, just like we came."

"You've already been to the clinic?"

"Yes."

"What about the psychologist?"

"Yes. Been there too. The doc prescribed meds that were supposed to help, but nothing works. Can you help me?"

As he talked, I remembered my dad telling about a similar experience he had as a sailor on the USS Yorktown during World War II.

"Doc, I want to tell you a story and then pray with you. Do you have time for that?"

"Uh, yeah! They're not letting me go anywhere or do anything, and if I'm not able to work by Wednesday I'm outta here. So yeah, I have time."

"My dad was a sailor during World War II. He joined the Navy to play clarinet in the Navy Band, but when Pearl Harbor was attacked, his ship immediately headed for the Pacific. After the Battle of Coral Sea, his fear was so real that my dad felt a heavy weight on his chest and shoulders. One night as the ship was sailing towards the Battle of Midway, he was lying on his bunk, fear like a heavy, paralyzing force making it almost impossible to breathe. He prayed out loud, *Lord I know I am saved, and it's OK if I die. But, God, take away this fear so I can do my job. Amen.* As soon as he finished praying, he felt the weight lift from his chest and shoulders. It was so real, he opened his eyes to look around to see if anyone had walked in. The fear lifted, and never returned.

"Doc, I'm going to pray for you, asking God to do the same thing for you that he did for my dad. These guys are going to be praying too. Are you ready?"

Tears had already started forming in his eyes. "Yes. I'm ready."

Several others overheard the conversation and gathered close by. They circled Doc and began to pray fervently. Mine was a rather simple prayer. "Lord, you have rescued many people from fear. You were there for my dad when he experienced this same fear during a different war in a different place. I ask, Lord, that you would set this man free from the fear, and put an end to his shakes, so he can do his job and finish the mission with his team. In Jesus's name. Amen." When we finished praying, we talked another ten or fifteen minutes, then the guys left. There was no noticeable difference in Doc's fear. He was still shaking.

I know not every prayer is answered the way we want, or when we want, and we usually don't know why. But I continued to pray for him throughout the day, and the next couple of days. He had said if the shakes didn't stop by Wednesday, then he'd be sent home, so Wednesday morning I went looking for him. I found him in his unit's command center, all dressed and outfitted to go out on patrol, standing next to his boss.

When Doc saw me enter the room, he yelled. "Chaplain! I've been meaning to come see you but got so busy. Sunday afternoon, about two hours after you prayed for me, I was in my hooch, lying on my bunk, trying to get some sleep, when all of a sudden, the shakes stopped and the fear was gone, and I slept through the night. Like about 14 hours. The next day I asked my boss if I could get back to work, but he told me, *Nope, not until you're seen by the docs and return with a written clearance.* So, I went over to the clinic. They ran a bunch of tests and determined that I'm OK. I haven't been shaking—not even once—since Sunday. God did for me the same thing he did for your dad."

We both had our battle rattle on, with all the armor inserts, which made hugging a little more awkward than usual. Even so, the hug between two Christian men was heartfelt; the spiritual connection and friendship were genuine. Then he said, "Chaps, our whole team wants to know if you'll pray with us before we go out again."

Before answering, I looked at the Lieutenant Colonel to make sure he approved. I can pray with anyone who voluntarily comes to see me. But I have to be careful not to impose on anyone who doesn't want anything to do with religion or prayer. It's a matter of respecting all people and all beliefs.

The commander, who had already become my friend, looked at me and said, "He's right, Chaplain. I told the guys that there was no expectation for them to be here when you prayed, but after hearing about what happened to Doc, several of them came to me and said they were coming voluntarily."

I prayed for their safety, for their families back home, and for their faith to be strengthened. Then they drove away. I would not see them for a week or so, depending on the weather and the war.

After they returned, they asked me to have lunch with the team. They showed pictures of the hummer that had been destroyed–the one they were pulled out of. It's amazing that any of them got out alive. Ordnance experts determined they had run over a triple IED—three times the explosive power of an ordinary explosive device. They should have all been killed. Looking at the pictures, you could hardly tell that the pile of scrap metal had been a vehicle. It's hard to fathom how anyone inside wasn't crushed or burned alive. How was it possible for them to be extricated from that burning heap? And yet, here they were. Not one of them afraid. Not one of them shaking.

CHAPTER 9

Rocket in the Clinic

When I entered the front door of the clinic the next afternoon, I encountered a silent, pale, zombie-like medical staff. They were usually upbeat, happy people who greeted everyone who went in. But today . . . not a word.

"What's going on?" I asked the guy at the front desk. The medical unit was staffed primarily by people from the Florida Army National Guard. University of Florida Gator paraphernalia decorated the wall behind him.

He looked at me and said, "Follow me."

As we walked, I wondered who died. I hadn't heard any sirens or explosions. What could possibly have happened?

He took me to the officer on duty, who was sitting behind his desk, also silent and ashen-faced. He stood up, his right palm facing up, his pointer finger beckoning me to follow. The only sound was our boots hitting the floor as we walked the long hall towards the back of the hospital. Then he stopped, staring at the wall, the same finger now guiding my line of sight to a large hole in the wall.

"What happened?"

"About an hour ago, I was on the phone arranging a medevac chopper for a wounded soldier when I heard *bang!* A rocket slammed through the wall, creating that hole, but it didn't explode. It travelled down this hall, ricocheting and caroming off the walls, the floor, and the ceiling. Look. You can see the scuffs and skids."

He was right. I saw the marks on the painted walls, the ceiling, and on the tile floor. A few spots were more like gouges than scuffs.

"It got down to the next hall and for some reason made a left turn, still bouncing all over the place. And then another left turn, right into my office, as if it had my name and address. It stopped on the floor in front of my desk, fan motor still whirring. I thought I was a dead man. I mean, that thing could go off any second. I said to the guy on the phone, *I gotta go*, and put the phone down. Holding my breath and waiting. Staring at the rocket on the floor. Listening to the buzz. Expecting the worst.

"The others came running in to see what happened. There are eight of us here today. They saw the rocket on the floor, fan still spinning and buzzing, me paralyzed behind the desk with a stupid look on my face. We're all in shock. That thing could have blown up the entire building, burned it to the ground, but it didn't go off."

One of the others continued the story.

"We walked away from the rocket, literally tiptoed out of the building, and called Ordnance. They came and looked at it, then took it out. It was still warm. Apparently, the wire connecting the detonator to the explosive came loose during flight, so even though it made a direct hit, it couldn't blow."

I spent a couple hours with the medical team that day. Several years earlier I had completed the Critical Incident Stress Management (CISM) training that the Army made available to chaplains. CISM includes a range of crisis intervention methods that usually include individual counseling, group debriefing, and post-incident referral for those who were either involved in a crisis or who watched someone else suffer or die. A chaplain will usually be a member of the response team rather than leading the team, but here at Camp Echo there were only two who were CISM trained—me and the psychologist—and he was gone for a couple of weeks, so it was just me.

The guys in the clinic definitely needed to talk and unload some stress after that incident with the unexploded rocket. They also needed to laugh. Some of them wanted to pray. With more casualties sure to come through those doors, we needed this team to be at their best all the time. And we couldn't afford to shut down the clinic and give them the day off. During war, it doesn't work that way. So, I followed up every day for the next few weeks.

Northern Iraq has a mild summer and a fair amount of rain, so trees are abundant. But it's a different story in the central and southern regions. Camp Echo was officially in the area called *MND-CS*, which stood for *Multi-National Division-Center South*. Here, not many trees survive without irrigation.

The most important tree is the date palm, which has been the national symbol of Iraq for thousands of years. Though there are more than 300 varieties of dates, most people are only familiar with the three or four common types that don't require much care or attention. These dates have been a dietary staple for Bedouins dating back to pre-Babylonian times, and are still the most important export other than oil, providing nutrition and income for millions of people.

Iraqis refer to the date palm as "the eternal plant" and "the tree of life." Up until the 1960's, people in the countryside used to hang lanterns at night from these trees to guide strangers to their homes. The lights indicated where travelers could find a meal and a place to sleep. According to tradition, any guest would be welcome to stay two or three days, even strangers.

The date palm is so important in Iraqi culture that it is taboo to harm it. An early Islamic leader in a military campaign once gave the order, "Do not kill a woman, a child, or an old man. And do not cut a tree."

During the 1980–1988 war with Iran, however, many trees were destroyed. Millions more date palms were killed by Saddam Hussein's agricultural policies. And during the second Gulf War, the U.S. Army bulldozed thousands of them, causing anger among the Iraqis that persists to this day.

Only two or three of the trees existed at Camp Echo, and a dozen or so wild fig trees. Nobody harvested them, so they were loaded with fruit, which attracted hundreds of birds.

The only birds we saw at Camp Echo were pigeons, which the locals called doves. The few trees we had at Camp Echo were filled with these pigeon-doves, who made a terrible cacophony throughout the day, and left their droppings wherever they very well chose. I theorized that all other birds were driven away by the rockets and mortars, which were also dropping wherever they very well pleased. Like the one that crashed through the wall of the medical clinic that morning.

As I walked away from the hospital, an Air Force *Combat Camera* friend of mine walked up to me and wanted to talk. The *Combat Camera* mission is to take pictures and videos which can be used for intelligence analysts, training, and PR. The Air Force also provides a pictorial historical record of America's military operations and involvement around the world. *Combat Camera* personnel are an integral part of joint exercises, contingency operations, humanitarian relief efforts, and disasters of every kind.

My friend had recently started attending Sunday worship, and we talked for a while about some of the things she was going through. Then she said, "Oh by the way, Chaplain, the Colonel wants to see you."

"OK. Thanks, Sergeant. I'll go over now. You coming?"

"Naw. My team's going out on a film project. Be gone the rest of the day, maybe not back til tomorrow afternoon."

"OK. Hope it goes well for you. I wanna see your video when you're done."

"You got it, Chaps."

When I walked into the Colonel's office, he told me he wanted me to go check on the MP's (Military Police). They'd been in town training the IP (Iraqi Police) when they were attacked. Two soldiers killed. "Yes, sir. I'm on my way." I went over to the MP compound prepared to engage in another CISM session.

It was a company-size element, about a hundred MP's, part of a battalion up in Baghdad. Their chaplain came down to Diwaniyah once a month to visit them, but I was there every day, and knew many of them. The First Sergeant met me at the entrance to their main building.

"Chaplain, two of my guys, young guys, popular, killed instantly. The company is in shock. Can you talk to 'em? Say somethin'?"

"Yeah, Top. I know what to do."

I walked into the training room, a simple rectangle about twenty-by-thirty feet lined with wooden benches, crammed with young soldiers. The older I get, the younger they get. These grieving young people had just watched two of their friends get shot, and then bleed to death. They were feeling anger, anguish, and angst.

It was too soon, though. They didn't want to talk to me. They wanted to be alone with each other as a team, as a unit, as friends. I spoke to them for about ten minutes, said a brief prayer, and then left. I would come back the next day.

I walked to my office and sent an email to their chaplain, a young Captain, asking if there were any chance he could get down to Camp Echo by tomorrow. I didn't know he was already on his way. When I got to the MP compound the next morning, he was there, lovingly caring for and ministering to his troops.

He and I had become friends a couple weeks earlier when he made his once-a-month visit to Camp Echo. He showed up in my office one day and asked, "Hey, can I take you out to lunch?"

"Sure. How 'bout Olive Garden?" We laughed, then walked over to the DFAC.

During lunch, he told me about his wife and four children, their home in Colorado, where he'd gone to college and seminary, and where he had been a pastor. I liked him right from the start. Five foot ten, slender, with short blond hair and bright blue eyes. He laughed readily, and cared deeply about people and his faith in God. He asked if we could go somewhere to talk privately.

"Sir, I need someone to talk to, someone to pray with."

"Sure, let's go back to my office. I think the air conditioner still works. I have some Diet Dr Pepper I can share with you." Once we got settled, he got serious.

"Sir, I've been here in Iraq three of the past five years, and I'm burned out. I have a wife and four kids. My first calling is to be a husband and father, and I need to be home with my family, but there's no telling when the Army will let me go home. I love being a chaplain, but I really miss my family."

I understood what my new friend was talking about. He was the kind of chaplain the Army needed: smart, spiritual, energetic, compassionate, and talented. But his family needed him, as well.

I was in a different season of life. My children were grown, and my wife was well into a successful career as a professor at a Christian university. Although she needed me and missed me, it wasn't the same as it was for a younger wife-and-mother with four young kids in the home. The sacrifices that he and his wife had to make in order for him to serve overseas were much more severe than the price my wife and I had to pay. Yet, here he was: serving, caring, ministering, and doing his job with faithfulness and excellence.

We got together whenever he was at Camp Echo. In the same way our medical staff was shaken by the rocket that slammed through the wall, went down the hall, and ended up in the office right in front of the doctor's desk, we were shaken by what we were facing day in and day out. We needed someone to talk with, pray with, and feel with. Being in Iraq during the war was tough.

The two of us were able to encourage each other, pray for one another, listen to what the other was going through, and in a very real way, bear each other's burden. I appreciated him, and started looking forward to his visits. I'm not sure he knows how much he did for me. The fellowship, pastoral care, friendship, and prayer were exactly what I needed.

CHAPTER 10

Inner Struggle

The generic danger that every soldier faces has been well chronicled. What makes it different is what goes on in the mind of each one of us. There are some common themes, of course, but the individual make-up, the personality, the background, and spiritual condition combine to make each story unique.

When I first got to Camp Echo, I had no issues, or so I thought, and I didn't expect to have any. I was "prayed-up," well-trained, eager to serve, and excited to be there. At fifty-two years of age, I was much older than most of the chaplains we sent over. That additional life experience, time in ministry, and maturity really helped.

However, it didn't take long for the environment and the experiences to start affecting me. Even though the Lord had used me to help others, occasionally the stress was overwhelming. I wasn't sleeping well. The daily mortars were taking a toll on my psyche.

The first inner anomaly that I noticed was a premonition that I was going to lose my right leg. It never happened, but the feeling was strong. So many mortars and rockets were landing inside the walls of the FOB, that I assumed one of them would have my name on it. Why should I be exempt? It happened to so many soldiers and Marines.

This sense of impending pain and loss was so real that I thought it might be a hunch or intuition from the Lord. Maybe it was a word from the Lord to prepare me for what was to come. I wonder if in a strange, psychological-sort-of-way I wanted something like that to happen. In any case, I got used to the idea and came to accept it.

Another emotion was new for me. I'd never experienced deep, long-lasting fear. Fear that doesn't stop when you go to sleep at night. Fear that wakes up with you in the morning. Fear that stalks you and haunts you. The same fear that my dad felt on the ship during WWII, and the same fear that gave the medic the shakes.

One day my assistant and I were eating lunch in the DFAC when we heard the sirens announcing incoming rockets or mortars. Immediately we got up and ran for the doors to get into the nearest bunker. As I reached the door, my Chaplain Assistant, Master Sergeant France, noticed something was wrong. She hollered above the noise of the crowded DFAC, "Chaplain, you don't have your Kevlar," and grabbed me by the collar, pulling me back inside. In a hurry to get out of there, I had forgotten that I didn't have my helmet on.

Just as she pulled me back inside and the door slammed shut, a mortar landed right outside. It's quite possible that she saved my life … or my leg. That could have been my turn to be hurt, but the alert Master Sergeant acted quickly and prevented it from happening.

During a Tuesday morning staff meeting, we were told that the terrorists in Diwaniyah were planning to attack Camp Echo. There were so many of them, and so few of us, it seemed they could easily take control of the FOB and kill or torture every one of us. To this day, I wonder whether the Colonel had his staff give us this warning merely as an incentive to stay alert. Maybe the enemy really was planning an attack. I don't know, but I took the threat seriously.

As a chaplain, I was a non-combatant. This means every other person on the FOB had a weapon; I was the only one who didn't. I wasn't even allowed to use a gun if I found one lying around and we were in a fire fight. When my Chaplain Assistant was injured and had to return to the States, I had no force protection assigned to me.

I started having nightmares in which I was captured by terrorists and tortured. I remember lying on my bunk worrying about this. When I mentioned it to the MiTT Team the next morning, the guys told me, "Don't worry, Chaps. You just stick close to us. We have enough fire power to take care of anything that might happen."

That was reassuring. They meant it, too. And they started checking on me whenever there was an incoming rocket or mortar. But I spent so much time away from them because I had to visit the clinic and other places on the FOB throughout the week, that I was still afraid of what might happen.

One time the sirens sounded in the middle of the night. I was so tired, that I decided just to stay in bed. Suddenly, one of the guys from the team pounded on the door. "Hey, Chaplain! You in there?"

"Yeah! Go Away!"

"You have to come to the bunker with us."

"No I don't. I'm staying in bed."

"Mortars are coming."

"I'm staying here. And if they land on my hooch and kill me, that's OK."

After pounding on the door and yelling at me some more, he finally left and went into the bunker. I didn't die that night, but the next day the Colonel chewed me out.

I was also lonely. How can you be lonely when there are more than 2,000 people nearby? But I was. I met some awesome people, and made some great friends while in Iraq. But I missed my wife, my sons, and my friends back home. It was wonderful to have people to spend time with, but they weren't from my own command, so I didn't know them very well.

Chaplain teams are sometimes "cross-leveled," meaning the Chaplain and Chaplain Assistant are plucked from their unit and dropped where they're needed, often with people they've never met and will never see again after the tour of duty is over. It's great ministry, wonderful camaraderie, and a good opportunity to meet new people, but the loneliness was inescapable, especially when conditions at Camp Echo started getting dangerous.

Along with loneliness comes sexual temptation. In 2007, Linda and I had been married 31 years and had been faithful to each other the entire time. I had determined early on in our marriage that I'd never cheat on my wife. But war has a way of breaking people. It weakens your willpower; it drowns out your values. Even when you're careful and intentional, the temptations can be strong.

I knew there was a strong current of sexual activity at camp Echo. Everyone was lonely. Everyone was needy. And we were all far from home. Right outside the DFAC, there was a large group of directional signs pointing towards hometowns, and displaying the number of miles away each city was.

||||||||||||||||||||||||||||||||||||||||||||||||||||||||||||||||||||||||||||||||||||||||||||||||||||||||||||||||

Savannah, GA: 6,785
Penn State, PA: 6,267
Charleston, SC: 6,632
Galveston, TX: 7,449
Westfield, MA: 5,975
Springfield, IL: 6,813

||||||||||||||||||||||||||||||||||||||||||||||||||||||||||||||||||||||||||||||||||||||||||||||||||||||||||||||||

There were signs for Los Angeles, San Diego, and Seattle. Calgary, Winnipeg, and Toronto. Signs for places in Europe and Australia, each sign showing how far we were from home. I lived in Atlanta at the time, so I was 6,839 miles from my wife.

A lot of people think when they're that far from home, and the circumstances are that bad, they're justified in doing things they wouldn't do otherwise. But instead of giving in to the temptations and the opportunities for sex or drugs or porn, I spent time with other Christian men, listened to Christian music, and worked out at the gym. I ate pecan pie a la mode and oatmeal raisin cookies, read my Bible and anything decent I could get my hands on. I prayed with some of the men who came to church or to one of the Bible studies. And I called home as often as I could.

Another struggle I had to deal with was anger. I was angry with the war, and angry because of the tragedy playing out in the lives and the families of those who were wounded or killed. Anger can be contagious, especially when you're exposed to so much of it over long periods of time. Were there valid reasons justifying this war, the cost in dollars, and the loss of human life? I don't know. It's not my place to determine whether our activities and our presence in Iraq were justified. That's a judgment call beyond my scope.

I never did lose my leg, and I'm thankful. But after I got home, I experienced depression that lasted almost a year. When the depression began to subside, I started having nightmares again. I dreamed about explosions, about people dying, about being captured by terrorists. I dreamed I was trapped and couldn't get away.

I've had mild claustrophobia for a while, but it got worse after being in Iraq. I was in our bedroom closet one morning. After getting a pair of pants and a shirt, I turned to leave, and my wife was standing in the doorway, wanting to talk to me. I experienced instant panic. "Get out of the way," I yelled. It wasn't a planned reaction. It just erupted.

In restaurants, I always looked for an escape route before sitting down. On the freeway, I made sure there was enough distance in front so if the traffic came to a standstill, I wouldn't be stuck. I was nervous every time someone followed too close behind me, whether on the road or walking down the sidewalk.

It took several years for me to learn how to control my response to feeling boxed in. It's still real, but enough time has elapsed, and I've worked at reminding myself that there's no danger anymore. Linda says I got to the point that the panic doesn't show, but she knows it's still there. Sometimes she wonders if it's going to erupt again.

Another result of being at Camp Echo during the war was the change in the way I eat. I used to relax during meals, and take my time. But when I got home, every time I ate, I'd wolf down the whole plateful of food in about a minute, and be ready to move on to something else. Being in the DFAC when mortars start raining from the sky teaches you not to linger. I still tell myself when having dinner with my wife, "Slow down, Paul. Do this for Linda. Enjoy the moment. Or at least fake it so she can enjoy it."

When I first got home, I'd hear a loud noise and duck for cover. A helicopter or plane would fly by, and instantly I was back in Iraq. Driving down the road, if there was something on the side of the road, I'd steer as far away from it as I could, a habit from the training they gave us about avoiding anything that might be an IED. In the MFA program at the University of Tampa, the assigned reading included a book about the war in the Middle East. I started reading, but the first few pages triggered a panic attack, and I had to put the book down.

Do I have PTSD? Definitely. Will it last forever? It might. Is it better than when I first got home? Oh, yeah.

As a chaplain, I didn't beg my boss to let me go to Iraq because I liked war or because I believed it was a just war. I wanted to be there because I knew there were people who needed a chaplain, people who at some point might want someone to pray with them, people who might be looking for guidance in how to become a Christian, people who needed someone to be strong for them, give them hope and courage, and represent Jesus Christ to them. I believe I did that, and I would do it again.

I hate to think how bad it might have been if I didn't have some good Christian men to talk with, pray with, and worship with while at Camp Echo. I am thankful for each of them. And I'm thankful for the faithfulness of God, who promised to never leave me nor forsake me. He kept his promise every day.

Chapter 11

Phone Call to Atlanta

I had invited the MiTT Commander to our Sunday worship services and Tuesday Bible studies many times, but he wouldn't come. I knew he was a member of a church back home, but he was too busy. Plus, it seemed like something inside him "broke" because of his experiences here.

A few weeks after we escaped being blown up by the "hotspot" at the intersection, he showed up in my office on a Thursday afternoon. Just walked in, sat in a chair, and started making small talk ... but he had a funny look on his face.

"Everything OK?" I asked. He was the commander and I was the chaplain, but we were the same rank, so we often used first names.

"I don't know how to say this, but I'll give it a try."

"What's up?"

"When we got back from town a few weeks ago, I was pretty shaken. I mean, if the drone hadn't been up there, or if it hadn't detected the IED, and if the guy hadn't radioed us to redirect us, we'd have been killed. There's a really good likelihood that I'd be dead. That all of us would be dead."

"I know. I've thought about that, too."

"That's been on my mind ever since. So, I called my mentor in my church back in Atlanta to talk. He's a deacon in the church, an older guy who kind of took me under his wing a couple years ago, and whenever I'm going through something or need someone to talk to or pray with, he's been there for me."

The seasoned military leader squirmed and fidgeted in his chair as he spoke. I didn't know what he was about to say, but I hoped we'd get through this conversation without incoming mortars forcing us out to the bunker.

"Well, when I called him last weekend to get some guidance, he told me about an article he read about a chaplain in Iraq. He said there's a chaplain over here who could help me. He didn't know where in Iraq this guy was, and Iraq is a big place, but if I could find him, that chaplain is the one to advise me and help me get my life back on track with God.

"So, I asked him what the guy's name was, and he said it was a chaplain named Paul Linzey, who's somewhere in Iraq. Said I should look him up, and wherever he is, go find him and talk with him."

I didn't know what to say, but the Major noticed a slight smile forming on my face. He smiled, too. Then he said. "Paul, you've been great. You've become a part of our team. You've invited me to church many times, and I keep refusing. Then this happens. I call all the way back to Atlanta for my mentor to tell me to go talk to my own chaplain at Camp Echo. So here I am."

A day or two after the *Eye-in-the-Sky* incident, I had written an article for my denomination's weekly magazine, and sent a copy to my boss at Fort McPherson in Atlanta, GA. I sent him the article because I thought he might want to hear about some of the things that were happening. I had no idea he would forward the email to the Public Relations Officer, who included it in the next command newsletter. The article told of healings, answers to prayer, people coming to faith in Christ, the *Eye-in-the-Sky* incident, plus a few other experiences. Some of the non-Christians in the command were understandably upset that the article was included in the newsletter. Another chaplain, who worked in Atlanta with us, shared the article with some members of his church. It just happened to be the same church this officer attended when he was home.

We talked about thirty minutes or so. About faith. About marriage. About the fact that he only smoked cigars while away from home with the Army because his wife can't stand 'em. About life and death. About why we're in this war.

Then, with a penitent and humble heart, he looked at me and said, "So, Padre, what do I need to do to get right with God?"

"My friend, I think you need to reaffirm your faith in the Lord, start participating in worship, ask the Lord to forgive you for the things you've done, and take some time every day—even if it's just a few minutes—to read your Bible and pray."

"OK. I can do that."

"I think you'll find that the Lord will encourage and strengthen you. He'll give you guidance and wisdom. You're already a good leader. Getting back to where you need to be spiritually will make you even more effective. Let's pray. You go first, and then I'll pray."

His prayer was simple, yet eloquent, asking for forgiveness and guidance, and thanking the Lord for his mentor back home in Atlanta. Then he pledged to be faithful to God in his personal life and in going to church. When I prayed, I thanked the Lord for the friendship we had developed, and for the way this encounter happened. I asked the Holy Spirit to pour his love into this man's life, to keep him safe until it was time to go home, and to help him start growing spiritually again.

After we prayed, he stood and shook my hand. "Thanks for being here. Thanks for writing that article and sending it back to Atlanta. And thanks for praying with me. I'll see you in church."

Sunday morning, he was there, sitting towards the back on my left. During the congregational singing, he stood quietly with both hands slightly raised to the Lord, and with tears in both eyes, he sang the songs of worship and praise.

He continued taking his team out on patrol. He faced danger day in and day out. I'm pretty sure he continued smoking those little cigars. They were one of the ways he handled the stress of being in Iraq. And he kept coming to church, raising both hands, both eyes moistened as he worshipped and gave thanks.

CHAPTER 12

Ping Pong with the Priest

The outer door of my office building opened, then slammed shut, followed by the sound of boots clomping down the hall, until they stopped at my door. I looked up to see Father Wlad dressed in camouflaged cargo-pocket shorts that reached below his knees, a faded pink-and-green floral buttoned shirt, greenish-brown combat boots that had seen better days, and thick, dark green, used-to-be-knee-high socks that had lost all elasticity so that they drooped down to the tops of his boots. His left hand held a table tennis racket. I burst out laughing at the apparition that filled the doorway.

"Want to play ping pong?" the priest asked.

"I'd love to," I managed to say, mentally rescheduling the tasks on my to-do list. I had been praying about Father Wlad the past few days, hoping for an opportunity to spend some time with him. He was faithful in his ministry as a Roman Catholic priest, conducting daily mass and confession, yet I sensed he needed a friend, just like I did.

We chatted as we walked over to the MWR, which was a combination gym and entertainment facility. The bottom level had weight machines and free weights. There were treadmills, stair climbers, ellipticals, and stationary bikes. The floor was concrete, and one side had a large, bright blue mat for floor exercises. Upstairs were pool tables, a stereo, books and magazines, card tables, sofas, and a humongous internal-projection big screen TV. In the center of the large, open, linoleum-covered area was a brand new, heavy-duty ping pong table. Father Wlad had planned this ambush, and had asked the MWR staff to reserve the table for our use.

"You never told me you play table tennis," I scolded.

"Table tennis is big in Europe. Everybody plays."

"Do you have a table in your parish hall back home?" I asked.

"Of course." It was like he was saying, "Silly American. Don't you know anything?"

Had I known there was to be a table tennis match today, I would have dressed for the occasion. I would love to have changed into my PT clothes. Instead, I was wearing my Army Combat Uniform with boots. What I wanted most was to be wearing athletic shoes.

Not having the right clothing wasn't my only worry, though. Europeans don't consider table tennis to be a casual game; it's a serious sport. Father Wlad had brought his personalized racket when he came to Iraq. I had to use whatever the MWR happened to have on hand, which wasn't as good as the equipment I used at home. Not only that, Wlad was left-handed, which presented a different set of dynamics to the game. This could get ugly.

We took about ten minutes to warm up, batting the ball back and forth to get a feel for each other's style of play. News spread quickly that the two chaplains were playing ping pong: Catholic versus Protestant, Polish versus American, Lefty versus Righty. By the time we began the first game, an audience of about twenty-five people had gathered to witness this international, interdenominational slugfest. They shouted, egged us on, and groaned or cheered with every shot and every miss.

The first player to 21 wins, but he has to win by at least two points. Father Wlad won the first game with a score of 21–10. It took me that long to figure him out—and to remember the coaching I had received as an 18-year-old freshman at San Diego State. An encounter with my cousin, Elmer, flashed into my mind.

Elmer, who was eight years older than I, invited me to have dinner with him and his wife, and while we were eating, he asked, "Do you play ping pong?"

"Sure."

"Are you any good?"

"Yeah, I'm pretty good. Why?"

"Well, I just bought a new ping pong table, but I've never played. S'pose you could teach me? Maybe show me a few things after dinner?"

"Sure. I'd be glad to."

After eating, we went out to the garage. I should have known as soon as we walked in that I was being set up. Brand new table, prominently placed in the center of the room. A rack on the wall held ping pong balls and paddles. Chairs for spectators along each side.

"Pick any paddle you want," Elmer graciously offered. Then he pulled a case from the shelf and took out his personal

*racket that nobody else was allowed to use . . . or touch . . .
ever!*

"So, how do you play this game?' he asked.

*After I gave a few of the basics, we got started. We played
ten games, and I never scored a point. He skunked me ten
times in a row, right after I told him I was pretty good.*

*"OK, cousin. I know two things about you. You're a great
ping pong player and a good liar."*

*After he stopped laughing, he said, "Don't ever call it ping
pong, Son. It's table tennis. And this is not a paddle, it's a
racket."*

"OK. Where did you learn to play . . . table tennis?"

*"I played in the Army, competed in the Servicemen's Table
Tennis Tournament in Germany several years, and even won
the thing once."*

*My cousin was a champion—a champion who apparently
delighted in taking advantage of his naïve, overconfident,
younger cousin. I learned later that he enjoyed pulling this
prank on many of his friends.*

*"So Elmer, s'pose you could teach me? Maybe show me a
few things?"*

"Sure. I'd be glad to."

*During the next few months, he taught me how to play the
game: the rules, the etiquette, technique, how to return spin
with spin, keep the ball rotating the same direction, unless,
of course, you decide to override the rotation of the ball with
power. Never touch the table. How to serve. The thickness of
the rubber on the racket. The guy knew the game inside and
out, and under his tutelage, I became a much better player.*

As Father Wlad started serving game two, suddenly, his serve, his spin, and his leftiness were not insurmountable. I won the second game 21–18. I also won games three, four, and five—each game by two or three points. The final game was long, going back and forth, neither of us able to get a 2-point lead for the victory until finally I beat him 32–30. We were exhausted. The Polish Catholic priest took the first game by 11 points. The American Protestant pastor took the next four games by a combined total of 10 points. So, he had more points, but I had more games. The fans cheered for both of us.

"Let's go back to my place for drinks," my opponent suggested.

"Sounds like a great way to spend an afternoon in Iraq," I replied." Then, thinking that he might only have beer, I asked, "Do you have any soft drinks?"

"Come. I will take care of you."

The Polish soldiers had built the chapel for Catholic mass and confession, but off to one side of the wooden structure, they added a large office and Father Wlad's living quarters. While I lived in an aluminum can, my compadre had a 600-square-foot, two-room apartment, complete with running water and a refrigerator. They knew how to take care of their priest.

Wlad went straight to the fridge, pulled out a beer for himself and a Diet Dr Pepper for me, smiling as he handed it to me. "See. I told you I take care of you."

I was impressed. Father Wlad had taken time to plan this day. The little store at Camp Echo didn't have my favorite drink very often. I had asked the manager if he'd order some Diet Dr Pepper once in a while, and he agreed. Whenever it was in stock, I bought a 12-pack or two. Wlad had gone over to the shop a week earlier to pick some up, knowing that's what I liked.

He lit a cigarette, put his feet up, and we spent the afternoon talking like old friends getting together for drinks at a roadside café somewhere in Europe. Father Wlad was from southern Poland, where he was a parish priest. His mom and dad were still living, as were his brother and sister. He had several nephews and nieces who adored him, wrote him letters, and sent pictures they drew. He pulled another beer and a Dr Pepper from the fridge.

"The chapel was hit by mortars before you got here," Wlad told me. "The fire burned it to the ground. My people built this chapel in its place. I've been here seven months, and I miss my home, my family, my friends, and my parish. Five more months to go."

"When you're done here, will you return to the same parish?"

"Yes. The bishop told me he is holding it for me. I am glad to go back to the same church."

"Wlad, I have a question for you."

"What's that?"

"Would you be willing to come to my Protestant service and let me interview you?"

"Come to your service? Why?"

"My Catholic soldiers attend your English mass, but my Protestants don't know you. Since you are the senior chaplain here, and you minister to my Catholics, and since we are a ministry team, I thought it might be a good idea for them to see us together. I've participated in several special masses already, but you haven't been to my services. Plus, you represent the Polish General, and my people need to know you, hear from you, talk with you. They need to know you are their chaplain, too."

Wlad leaned back in his chair and thought for a minute. He wasn't sure about this. "Would you give me a list of questions in English so I can practice?"

"Yes, I can do that. How much time do you want?"

"Two weeks, maybe? At least two weeks."

"I'll bring the questions tomorrow, and you can tell me when you're ready."

After talking a while longer, we had to take cover in a bunker because of incoming mortars. "Shall we go over to the clinic together to see if there are injuries?" I suggested.

"Good idea," my friend answered.

I returned the next morning to deliver a list of nineteen questions, but Wlad wasn't there, so I left the list on his desk. When I saw him in the DFAC that evening, he told me he got the questions, and that he'd be ready in two weeks.

"I am excited about it." He told me. "I think it'll be fun."

"Me too, Wlad."

Telling people that the Catholic priest would be attending Protestant worship generated a lot of interest. I realized that there might be too many people to fit into the small chapel. I'd been thinking about moving worship to the theater anyway because it would hold more than 150 people. This could be the kick-off for the new location.

My volunteer assistants created flyers and posted them all over the base: the laundry building, the post office, the store, the DFAC, the barber shop, the command HQ, all the restrooms and shower trailers, and in every building that had a bulletin board.

When the day arrived, more than 200 people showed up for church in the theater: Father Wlad's congregation of 50 Catholics, my 45 Protestants, and more than a hundred who didn't participate in either group. There were Croatians, Ukrainians, Poles, Americans, British, Spaniards, Australians, Germans, and a gentleman from India. Most of the attendees were military, but several civilians were there, as well. Most spoke English. When the

150 seats were taken, the rest had to stand in the back and on the sides of the room.

Pastor James opened with prayer and welcomed the group. We sang three songs. Then I introduced Father Wlad and began the interview.

1. Where were you born?
2. Where did you live as a child?
3. What activities did you enjoy when you were young?
4. Describe your family and some of your childhood experiences.
5. What is your favorite food?
6. When did you start attending church?
7. When did you begin to understand that the Lord was calling you to the priesthood?
8. How did that happen?
9. What do you like most about being in the ministry?
10. Do you have a favorite Scripture?
11. What do you like about God?
12. As an adult, what activities do you enjoy?
13. Is a priest's life lonely sometimes?
14. Who are your close friends?
15. How long have you been in the Army?
16. Were you a parish priest before the Army?
17. How much longer will you be in the Army?
18. Then what will you do?
19. Is there anything else you would like to tell us?

He was well-prepared. His responses to the questions were rehearsed, displaying a wonderful sense of humor that had everyone laughing several times. He told stories of his childhood, including the times he got into trouble. He mentioned his teen years, his dating experiences before becoming a priest. That surprised everyone. He talked of family life with his parents and siblings, and included anecdotes of his early years in the priesthood. He was a real character and an accomplished entertainer, his accented English adding to the performance. The crowd loved him, and so did I.

When we concluded the interview, the audience gave him a standing ovation. He was the star of the show. And after Pastor James said the benediction, at least forty soldiers from several nations mobbed Father Wlad. They wanted to talk to him, touch him, and hear more of his stories They wanted this moment to last a little longer.

When the last of them left the theater, Wlad turned to me and said, "Now I have a surprise for you. Once a month we have special food from Poland in our dining area. Would you join me for lunch?"

"That sounds great. I'd love to."

He introduced me to the Polish officers who were in the lunch room, including his General, then told me about the different foods on the menu for that day. Two kinds of soup, bread like the people in Wlad's hometown would make, and several types of pastries for dessert. I could tell that it was special for these men to have food from their homeland, even if only once a month.

Wlad selected a corner table where we could talk privately. "I have to tell you what happened to me while I was preparing for the interview," he said. "The questions brought back so many memories and emotions. When I got to number nine and number eleven, I remembered what it was back then that made me want to be a priest—a sense of God's love and his reality. And while I was writing my answers, I stopped and prayed, renewing my faith in God, and my commitment to serving him."

CHAPTER 13

Croatians at the Bible Study

My college history professor was eight years old when his parents moved the family to a small village in Africa to serve as missionaries. After being there a year, his father went to the tribal chief to ask why he and his people refused to listen to the message, and why they wouldn't come to church. The chief looked at the missionary and said, "We have a tradition. When you put into your mouth what we put into our mouth, then we will listen to what comes out of your mouth." The chief knew that during their first year in the village, the Americans insisted on eating food that they had brought with them, and avoided the local "cuisine."

After hearing what the chief said that day, the missionary went home and told his family that from then on, they would be eating what the village people ate, which consisted mostly of roaches and other insects. A short time later, the village chief came to church, listened to what came out of the missionary's mouth, and became a Christian. Within a few months, the entire village had converted to Christ.

My professor finished the story by telling us, "You know, it's amazing. Roasted roaches taste a lot like almonds, and they have that … crunch." A smile covered his face as he finished the story.

Missionaries around the world have to make some drastic lifestyle changes and sacrifices if they are to be effective in communicating with people of other cultures, traditions, and world views. And as our professor related to us, even the children of missionaries have a price to pay and sacrifices to make.

It's for similar reasons that many denominations organize military chaplains as part of their missions departments. An effective missionary will eat what the people eat, dress how they dress, speak their language, learn their culture, live among them, and endure the same conditions as the people they serve, all for the privilege of representing Jesus Christ and speaking into their lives with the Gospel. Chaplains do the same thing.

As an Army chaplain, I dressed in the same uniform every soldier wore. When they ate a prepackaged *Meal, Ready to Eat*, I had an MRE for dinner. I went wherever my soldiers went, even if that meant sleeping on the ground or road marching in the rain or dodging mortars in the desert.

The Army has its own lingo consisting of words, phrases, acronyms, and unique terminology known only to soldiers. Chaplains have to know this specialized lingo just like everyone else in the military. It's recommended that chaplains don't swear like their soldiers, sailors, airmen, or Marines, but we do have to understand what they're saying, and that it's part of the culture. Also, we can't react negatively to everything non-Christians do or say.

Earlier in my career, I was assigned to an infantry battalion. The day I showed up and started meeting some of the guys, the Sergeant Major introduced himself and asked, "Hey Chaplain, do you have your *Gotcha Cards?*"

"No, Sergeant Major. I've never heard of a *Gotcha Card*, and don't know what it is, so I'm pretty sure I don't have one. What is it?"

"The chaplain we had a couple years ago, every time he heard one of us cuss or swear or use the Lord's name in vain, he'd pull out a business card, but all it said in big bold letters was *Gotcha.*

"So, when the guys heard we were getting a new chaplain, they started wondering if you were going to be like the last one."

"I bet you guys hated him."

"Yes. We. Did."

"Tell you what. I don't plan on having any *Gotcha Cards* printed up, so you can relax. Cuss if you want. I'm here to love you guys."

Apparently, a bunch of soldiers were listening to the conversation, because as soon as I made that last statement, a cheer erupted from around the corner.

"You're gonna fit in fine here, Chaps. Nice to have you aboard."

Part of the training required of every soldier is what we call "NBC Training." NBC is an acronym for *Nuclear, Biological, Chemical* training. It's sometimes referred to as CBRN training: *Chemical, Biological, Radiological, and Nuclear.* Whatever you call it, it is one of the worst training experiences a soldier will ever face.

When I was in the Chaplain Officer Basic Course at Fort Monmouth, NJ, back in 1991, they put us in a bus and took us out to the woods of Fort Dix for a couple weeks. We marched, checked each other for ticks, dug trenches, and completed the obstacle courses. One day they lined us up near the entrance of a windowless, cement building: one door in, one door out. While standing in line outside, we got the order to put on our NBC uniform, which consisted of thick, specially-made, impenetrable pants and overcoat, rubber boots and gloves, and a gas mask. Oops! They told us never to call it a gas mask. It's a "protective mask." When all of us were suited up, the Sergeant yelled and barked our instructions.

"When I give the order, you will remove your protective mask. You will remain at attention. When I give the signal, you will state your name, rank, Social Security number, and your home address. And just in case you think you can hold your breath long enough to escape the pain, you will then recite the Soldier's Creed. You are not to leave the NBC training environment until told to do so. Is that clear?"

"Yes, Sergeant!" All of us shouted in unison.

We had heard the horror stories. Now we were about to experience it first-hand. They marched us into the gas chamber twelve at a time, and we stood at attention in a straight line, as directed.

When the Sergeant gave the command, we ripped off the masks, instantly feeling the burning of the gas on our skin, in our eyes, in our nostrils and mouths. Half of the guys in our group puked; the rest of us gagged, cried, spit, and coughed, doing our best to shout our name, rank, Social Security number, and address. Then we all ran for the door, not waiting for the Sergeant's permission, not bothering to recite the Soldier's Creed. We heard his words, "GET BACK IN HERE!" Then he cussed and called us names, but not one of us obeyed. We were gone! Still vomiting. Still gagging. Still crying.

The chemicals used in the NBC training are designed to give us confidence in our equipment, and the process works. While wearing the suit and mask, we didn't even know there were chemicals in the air, but as soon as the masks came off, wow! We do that NBC training almost every year because we have to make sure each person in the military is prepared for a chemical attack.

Chaplains are not exempt. This was part of the price I had to pay for the privilege of serving the troops, representing God and my church to men and women who might never spend time with a pastor otherwise. It was a sacrifice I gladly made because I loved my soldiers and was determined to be there when they were ready to talk about the Lord, when they wanted prayer, or when they needed counseling.

Another sacrifice is the twice-a-year Army Physical Fitness Test (APFT). Soldiers train year-round so they are always in great shape, but we're tested in the spring and in the fall. When I was in the Army, the APFT consisted of push-ups, sit-ups, and the two-mile run, followed by a weigh-in. Any soldier who failed to stay in shape was in danger of being discharged.

I know several chaplains who were kicked out of the military because they didn't comply with the weight standards, or couldn't pass one of the tested events. Just as we have to maintain ordination with our faith group, we have to pass the physical standards if we are to maintain the right to minister in the military.

I've mentored chaplains who balked at this, but I told them, "Listen. If you feel God's calling on your life to be a chaplain in the Army, then you have the responsibility to stay in shape and successfully complete the APFT. If you don't, then either it's not God's calling, or you are disobeying the Lord. It's simply one of the requirements for serving. Get out there and run. Do the push-ups. Do the sit-ups. Or get out of the Army and serve the Lord somewhere else."

There are seven qualifications for every pastor, priest, rabbi, imam, or theological student who desires to become a military chaplain: Education, Citizenship, Ministry Experience, Security/ Background Check, Medical Exam, Ordination, and Physical Fitness. Every one of these is also a potential disqualifier, which means as far as the military is concerned, it doesn't matter how good a preacher or counselor you are, if you aren't ordained or don't pass your medical exam, you're not going to be a chaplain. If you can't do push-ups, sit-ups, and the two-mile run, forget about it.

The words of the village chief to the missionary are true for the military also. "When you put into your mouth what we put into our mouth, then we will listen to what comes out of your mouth." And by extension, "When you live according to the same standards the rest of us in the military have to live by, then you earn the right to speak into our lives."

That's how a chaplain becomes a missionary to our military. That's how we get a foot in the door in terms of earning their trust. That's what it takes to serve our soldiers, sailors, airmen, Coast Guardsmen, and Marines.

But the way we do war nowadays, with multiple partner nations forming a coalition, we sometimes have an opportunity to minister to people from all over the world. I've already mentioned the Ukrainian officer whose eyes were healed and who then converted to Christ. I've introduced you to my friend, Father Wladislaw. But there were others, too.

A lot of people attended church the morning I interviewed Father Wlad. Some were not members of any organized religion, but hearing that Protestants and Catholics were getting together piqued their curiosity. That was new to them. Strange. So, they came. Two days later, two Croatian officers showed up in the conference room where I conducted the Tuesday evening Bible study. The one who spoke English explained, "We were there Sunday morning and had never seen church like that before. The way you do it was fresh. We want to hear more about your God and the Bible."

"Does your partner speak English?" I asked.

"No. She is my commanding officer, and she speaks Croatian. Not English."

I ran to my office across the hall. Fortunately, my computer was on. The discussion that night focused on Philippians chapter two, so I opened up Biblegateway.com and printed the chapter in Croatian and English, then returned to the conference room, handing the scriptures to my guests.

The English-speaking Croatian looked at both pages and was delighted to have the scripture in both languages. He served as translator for his boss during the Bible study, and towards the end of the discussion, both of them asked Christ into their lives as Lord and Savior.

I began to realize that though I was there specifically to serve American military personnel, a side benefit was the opportunity to impact civilians and military from fourteen nations.

I think there's a truth here for Christians in any career field. If you do your job well, if you are friendly towards people, if you pray regularly and live a consistent, godly life, the Lord will open doors for you. You can have a meaningful impact for the Kingdom without annoying or alienating people. You don't have to condemn them or hand them a *Gotcha Card*. Just love them and care about them. The Holy Spirit will take care of the rest.

CHAPTER 14

Running in the Dark

At one point, near the end of my deployment, I had a lengthy report to send up to Camp Victory so my supervisory chaplain would know where we stood in terms of establishing the religious program at Camp Echo. As soon as it was up and running, he would be able to make the case to his boss to send a permanent chaplain team. So, I was working late, putting everything I could think of into the report.

Things were going really well. Within two months, we had moved from the little Polish Catholic chapel at the far end of the FOB into the larger base theater. It was a lot closer to the housing areas, was a neutral facility, and facilitated the growing congregation. Sunday morning attendance now averaged almost 50 people. We had two offices and access to a conference room for meetings and counseling. There were twelve small-group fellowships and Bible studies meeting throughout the FOB, led by men and women I had trained or approved. I felt good about our progress.

An early goal of mine was to visit every office and unit each week. It was an ambitious schedule, but as a result of that regular face-to-face interaction, I had a fantastic relationship with the people on post, even with those who had no intention of attending worship. Pastor James played an important role in making that happen, and because of the rapport with the key players, I had an open door whenever I needed to talk to a soldier and whenever I needed help. It was an amazing community of effective teamwork that made serving and ministering there meaningful and fun. Friendship really does lead to ministry. Investing in people pays off in many ways.

Before finishing the report, I decided to call my supervisory chaplain up in Baghdad. I knew he tended to work long hours, too, and thought he might pick up the phone. I had a couple of questions to ask, but I also wanted to tell him personally some of the great stuff that was happening that would never go into the paperwork.

The official report asked for numbers, accomplishments, and challenges. I had to give the number of people attending worship, but not the number of converts. My denominational endorser's report asked for that kind of information, but the military reports do not. There was a box to write the number of counseling sessions, but not the number of answered prayers.

When I told him what was happening, he said, "What are you? A flaming evangelist? You got a real revival going on down there? I've been a chaplain in the Army over twenty-six years, and I've never seen that sort of stuff happen. A lot of chaplains have never led a soldier to faith in Christ. What are you doing?"

"Well, sir, I go around loving people, then I pray for them, and God does stuff. It is rather extraordinary."

He went on. "My goodness. People getting saved every week. Soldiers and Marines healed. Prayers being answered."

"Yes, sir. That's what's happening. I plan to send the report tonight, but this sort of stuff isn't in the report. I just wanted you to know about it."

"Well, thanks for the phone call."

As I was finishing up the report, the telephone rang. It was one of the medics at the clinic. "Chaplain, can you get over here, like right now? We just had a truckload of people come in, many of them hurt bad. Looks like two or three might not make it, and they've asked to see a chaplain." The report would have to wait til tomorrow.

My usual route to the clinic was out the front door of the building, down a side path to Main Street, and over to the alley behind the clinic. I had walked and run that route many times. Sensing the urgency of this situation, however, I decided to try a shortcut someone had told me about. It would take me behind and between buildings, and across the wooden veranda between the commander's office and his meeting room. The problem was that there was absolutely zero light out that night. None. For security reasons, we didn't have area lights on the FOB. The moon was in some other galaxy. The darkness was total. Yet I ran.

On the way there, I had a really strong hunch that I should stop running. More than just a sense that sprinting in total darkness might not be a very smart thing to do, it was like there was an inner voice shouting at me, "STOP RIGHT NOW!" So, I did. I stopped running and simply stood there in the dark.

In the black of the night, feeling rather stupid, wondering what to do next, I reached out in front of me. That's when I bashed my hand against a wooden barrier literally two inches in front of my face. Had I not listened to that inner voice, I would have smacked right into that wall running full speed. Moving my hands along the wood and picking up a splinter in the process, I found the end of the board, went around it, and walked blindly to the clinic.

A convoy of our people returning from a FOB near Najaf had been attacked. Somewhere along the 50-mile journey, they were visible and vulnerable. Our medical team would be working all night trying to save as many lives as possible. I talked and prayed with the wounded who were conscious. I prayed for those who were not. I would come back in the morning, but most would already be medevac'd to Baghdad or Germany by then.

The next day I went back to the temporary wall where I had stopped cold the night before, and saw that it had been placed right in front of a walkway leading to the rear entrance of the command center. While I was standing there looking at the wall, the Colonel walked up.

"Hi, chaps. Whatcha lookin' at?"

"Good Morning, sir. How long has this wall been here? I don't remember seeing it before?"

"We've had so many people taking a shortcut through here and coming in the back door of my office building without knocking. So, I had this barrier put up yesterday to keep people from coming through here. Seems to be working so far. Nobody's tried to come in the back door since we put it up."

"I guess not," I said. "Looks like a pretty effective way to stop foot traffic."

"Yup."

"No announcement or notification at staff meeting about the wall?"

"No, Chaplain. I wanted to surprise those who haven't been paying attention. I've been telling people for weeks to use the other door, and they keep coming through here, all hours of the day and night."

I told him what had happened the night before.

"Man! I should have told you."

"Not a problem, sir. The Lord told me."

"Well, Chaplain, if anyone's listening to God around here, it should be you. Say, I heard you're being promoted to Lieutenant Colonel?"

"Yes, sir. That's one of the things I want to talk with you about. I'd like to know if you'd participate in the ceremony."

"I'd like that. Send me the date and the details of what you want. By the way, how much longer are you going to be here? I'm hoping you'll be here the entire time I'm here."

"Well, sir, that depends on the MNC-I chaplain and my supervisor back home. I just sent a report letting them know that the religious program is up and running, and that whenever they're able to get a permanent chaplain team, you're ready. So, I imagine you'll be hearing from MNC-I within a month, is my guess."

"Mind if I recommend that he let you stay the rest of the year?"

"Sir, that's nice to hear. Thank you. However, my boss at Fort MacPherson wants me back ASAP. He would have to sign off on any request for extension."

"Well, you can't blame me for asking, right?"

"No sir. It would be a privilege to stay longer. We'll find out soon how long it'll be."

"Awright, Chaps. And no more running in the dark!"

"Ha! Yeah, right! I mean, yes, sir!"

CHAPTER 15

Laundry Building Bombed

The next morning started with a bang ... literally. Instead of the usual mortars, two rockets landed almost simultaneously. One exploded in our motor pool fuel yard, blowing up several large containers of gasoline or oil, creating flames that shot up twenty feet into the air. The other fell directly on our laundry building, which was encased in a 12-foot-high concrete wall.

Two civilian women, both from Texas, were inside. The first was a forty-four-year-old woman who had a husband and two kids in high school back home. She worked for the military the past three years. The other was an eighteen-year-old who arrived two weeks earlier: just out of high school, her very first job. Friendly. Funny. Nice young lady. She liked being around the older woman, who she looked up to and thought of as a mother figure.

They were sitting on the counter talking at 7:39 AM, ready to unlock the doors at 8:00, when the missile smashed through the ceiling and landed on the floor right in front of them. Unlike the rocket that entered the medical clinic and refused to detonate, this one exploded as soon as it hit the floor, killing both women instantly. They didn't stand a chance.

In my hooch getting dressed and ready for the day, I heard the now-recognizable high-pitched whistle of a 240-millimeter rocket. It sounded dangerously close. I'd not heard one that loud before, and wondered if it flew directly overhead. I ran out to the bunker, barely getting inside before the explosions.

As soon as I heard the all-clear, I ran over to see where it landed and if anyone was hurt. I found two soldiers from my MiTT Team wandering around in a daze. The Major and the Master Sergeant were on their way to a meeting when the laundry building took the direct hit. Even though they were on the opposite side of the concrete wall surrounding the laundry facility, the explosion knocked them to the ground. They didn't take any shrapnel, but they couldn't hear very well.

I yelled at them, "You need to see a doctor."

"What?"

"You need to see a doctor."

"No, we're OK."

"You have to go to the clinic!"

"No. We don't. We're OK."

"It's not an option. You are going to the clinic even if I have to drag you there."

I took both of them by the arm and escorted them the several block's distance to the medical clinic, where they were examined. Both sustained partial hearing loss, and both suffered some degree of Traumatic Brain Injury from the concussion. How severe and long-lasting the damage was would be determined later, but both were back at work within two days, ready to complete the mission. Later, both of them received the Purple Heart.

When I went back to the laundry area, I saw that everything made of wood or cloth had burned, leaving a rubble of corrugated aluminum roofing, steel frame, and roof supports that were still trying to stand, but had melted and bent under the weight of the roof and the heat of the fire. Strewn about the smoldering pile were the charred air conditioners, washers, and dryers. There were no remnants of clothing, and no remains of the women.

During war, there is a juxtaposition of tragedy and practicality, life and death, wanting everything to stop, yet having to go on. I conducted the memorial ceremony and grieved with everyone else at the FOB. Then we had to get back to work.

I had five sets of Army Combat Uniforms when I got to Camp Echo. Four of them were in the laundry when it burned to the ground. I should have picked them up a day or two earlier, but I was too busy and forgot to get them. Also in the laundry were my socks, underwear, workout clothes, and a few items of casual wear. All I had left was one uniform, boots, running shoes, a couple pair of socks, and one or two pairs of underwear.

Our little store didn't carry uniforms or clothing of any kind, so I had to order some, and have it shipped. I emailed my wife and she sent more clothes, but it would take weeks for the package to get from Atlanta to Iraq. Worse, it would be months before a new laundry facility would be built. How was I going to do my laundry in the meantime? I didn't have to wonder long. Two days later, Father Wlad came to my office.

"I will do your laundry," he announced.

"How will you do that?" I questioned his ability as well as his sanity.

"I have washing machine in my home. I brought it with me from Poland."

"You're kidding! You brought a washing machine to Iraq?"

"Hey! Even during war we have to have clean clothes, and I didn't know if we would have laundry, so I brought it from home. Yes. Go get your dirty laundry and meet me at my place."

When I got there, Wlad led me around the side of the chapel where a makeshift shed had been built. An extension cord drooped overhead between the chapel and the shed. A thinner-than-usual water hose ran from a window, along the sand, and up into a small washing machine that Wlad had pulled out of the shed.

"Give me your laundry, please. You not use my machine. I will wash your clothes. I am your servant."

I handed the laundry bag to the priest, who hand fed my garments into the machine. He used the hose to fill the tub with water, then plugged in the extension cord, and the contraption came to life.

"It wasn't easy to get this machine here. I had to talk to a lot of people. And then when I got here, I had to persuade them to bring electricity out here to the shed. But they did, and it works."

"Inside your apartment there's a refrigerator, and out here a washing machine?"

"Yes, my friend. Just a few simple necessities," he smiled.

When the wash cycle was finished, he took my clothes, wrung out as much water as he could, and hung them on the makeshift clothesline that sagged parallel with the extension cord.

"You go back to work. Come back later in the day, and your things will be dry."

"Thank you, my friend. I have to spend some time with my Military Intelligence unit this afternoon, so I'll come back maybe after dinner."

In the command staff meeting that morning I learned that our Military Intelligence (MI) team had been ambushed. Twenty of them had gone to another FOB, and on their way back, the lead truck ran over an Improvised Explosive Device. Sometimes an IED is detonated by a cell phone, other times by running over a rubber tube, which uses the compressed air to push a button, setting it off. Some explosives are like homemade land mines, rigged to blow as soon as weight is applied to the pressure plate. This one had a trip wire.

When the first vehicle blew up and burst into flames, two people in the front seat died immediately, and the five-truck convoy came to a halt. The soldiers in the trucks jumped out of their vehicles to help their comrades, not knowing there were a dozen snipers hiding in and on top of the nearby buildings. Four Americans were shot and killed; the other 14 took cover under their trucks, hoping somehow they would survive. The unseen shooters fired at them for the next thirty minutes. Three more were wounded.

It took hours for additional Coalition Forces to arrive and rescue them. I was in their training room when the survivors of the ambush returned to Camp Echo. Those in their unit who had stayed behind joined us. Because they hadn't gone on this trip, they were angry, feeling that they might have been able to help had they been there. I talked with them as a group for over two hours. They were traumatized, not only because of what they'd just experienced. What made it worse was that these soldiers had never lost anyone from their group before. Never had a friend or someone they worked with been killed or even injured. They'd been lucky. Until now, they didn't know what it was like to have a team member or a friend die.

They talked. They cried. They cursed. They yelled. They wanted revenge. They grieved. Some paced the floor. Others slunk in their chairs. They were experiencing Kubler-Ross's five stages of grief at an accelerated rate–Denial, Anger, Bargaining, Depression, and Acceptance. We were more than an hour into the session when one of them said, "Chaplain, can we pray?"

"Definitely. We can do that. But to honor those who may not want to pray, let's take a 10-minute break. Then anyone who wants to may come back here and we'll pray."

During the break, a few went to the restrooms. Some went out to smoke or get something to drink. Most stayed in the training area and wanted to keep talking. After ten minutes, every one of them was back—all of them—and wanted to participate in the prayer. Some of them volunteered to pray. They prayed for their friends who had just been killed. For the three who were wounded. They prayed that this terrible war would be over soon so no one else would have to die needlessly. They prayed that they'd be able to stay focused and do their jobs, even though they hurt so badly. Two of them, without being prompted asked Jesus to come into their hearts, as Lord and Savior.

When I prayed, I asked the Lord to comfort them as they grieved, that God would help them sort through the emotions they were experiencing, that they would be able to focus on their work, and that they would make the most of the friendships they had. I finished with a benediction, and invited them to call me or come see me any time they wanted to talk.

One tall, skinny soldier who seemed to be 19 or 20 years old, asked if he could talk with me right now. After the room cleared, he said, "I'm a Mormon. I know you're not an LDS chaplain, but would you pray with me anyway?"

"Of course, I'll pray with you. Be glad to," I answered.

Afterwards, I told him of a brand-new Latter-Day Saints sacrament service that had formed on post, and that there were two bishops leading the group. He was thrilled to hear that he would be able to worship and fellowship with people from his own faith group.

Before leaving, I stepped into the MI leader's office and closed the door. The commander and the senior NCO looked at me. "Are you guys OK?" I asked softly.

"It's been a tough day," one of them said.

"We've never had a casualty," the other added. "This makes the war real—real fast."

"I want you guys to know that I'm here for you, too," I told them. "Even leaders have emotional and spiritual needs."

"Thanks, Chaps. Come back and visit our people in a day or two, will ya?"

"I will."

When I returned to the chapel a few hours later to check on my laundry, Father Wlad had taken my clothes from the line, and folded them for me.

"Wow!" I said. "Saying 'thank you' doesn't seem to express how grateful I am. That is so kind of you. You have become a good friend, Wlad."

"No, I am doing this to thank you for what you have done for me. Because of your friendship, I have renewed my faith in God and the commitment to my calling as a priest. God sent you to Iraq and Camp Echo just for me."

Hearing Wlad say that was a confirmation that I had done the right thing in asking to deploy, that this was exactly where I was supposed to be. Before coming, I had no idea what the Lord had in mind, the people whose lives he was already working in, who just needed someone to represent the Lord to them. Someone who

CHAPTER 16

The Blue Book

Father Wladislaw's right-hand man, his "altar boy," was a civilian from India who worked in the DFAC. About fifty years of age, his name was Valrie. We came to know each other because I had attended several of Father Wlad's special masses when he hosted the Military Bishop of Poland. Poland has a long history with many significant events and holy days throughout the year, so the priest had a special-occasion mass almost every week. By now, we were pretty close friends, and he wanted me to participate in each special mass. It was on these occasions that the priest's assistant and I got to know each other.

We saw each other on post from time to time, also, and I would sometimes stop by the DFAC between meals to talk with him. He was a good guy, faithful in his duties for the priest and for the Lord. I noticed after a while, that after Catholic mass was over, he tended to stay at the church, even after we began the Protestant worship service.

I dropped into the DFAC one afternoon to get something to drink when the temperatures were again pushing past 120 degrees. The altar boy from India greeted me warmly and asked if we could talk privately. We each got a drink, then he led me to a back room, sort of like a private dining room that I had never seen, and closed the door.

"Chaplain Paul, for the past three weeks, I have stayed longer after mass to clean up and put things away. But the real reason was so I could listen to your services, your sermons. The way you teach the Bible, and the way you talk about Jesus … it's like you know him. And I have never heard anyone talk about the Bible or Jesus like that. I want to know more. I want to go home to my family and tell them about the things I have heard you talk about. And I want to buy the blue book."

"The blue book?" I wasn't sure what he was asking about.

"Yes. I have seen you carrying a blue book, and I've seen you teach from it. Where can I get the blue book?"

"Oh! That isn't a book you can buy. I wrote it for my church Bible study back home, and I brought it to use for the Bible studies and sermons here."

I could see his disappointment when I said the book was not available. Then an idea popped into my head. "Would you like me to photocopy the book and give it to you?"

"Yes. Yes. Please. It would mean so much to me and my family and my friends. I have been away from home the past 27 years. I see my wife and my children once a year when I go home for Christmas. But there are no jobs in our city. The only way I can provide for them is to find work wherever I can around the world, and send the money to my wife. My children have grown up without me. Now I am getting older, and next year I want to go home to stay. I want to talk about the Bible and Jesus the way you do. I want to tell my family and my friends that he is real. Maybe I will start a Bible study in my home."

The next morning, I copied the blue notebook containing my notes on Paul's letter to the Philippians, and gave it to him. I also gave him a copy of the devotional book by Henry and Richard Blackaby, *Experiencing God Day-by-Day*, that I provided for my soldiers. He took the books, shook my hand, and thanked me.

"With these materials, I can teach my family about Jesus." He beamed.

"You're still going to be Father Wlad's altar boy, right?"

"Yes, of course. I will be faithful."

"Good. I'll talk to you again soon."

"But, is it OK for me to keep coming to your meetings, too?"

"Of course, you may. You are always welcome. But please tell Father Wlad what you are doing. He needs to know."

"Thank you. I will see you soon."

I came to Iraq hoping to make a difference for American service personnel, and the Lord graciously allowed me to do that. I ministered, counseled, encouraged, and befriended airmen from South Dakota, Ohio, and New York; Marines from California, Kentucky, and Oregon; sailors from Maryland and Alabama; police officers from Pennsylvania, Washington, and Georgia; an FBI agent from Virginia; and soldiers from almost every state in the Union.

The surprise was that I also had opportunity to speak into people's lives from other places as well: Poland, Ukraine, Croatia, Iraq, and India. Some British soldiers attended our services, and a few from Australia and Canada, Romania and Spain. These men and women from the coalition nations returned to their countries, hometowns, and families, taking the experiences and stories of what God did for them in Iraq.

I still have the blue book. Someday, I would love to visit the priest's assistant and the Bible study he wanted to start when he went home to India. I'd love to find out if he was able to use his copy of the blue book to talk about Jesus with his wife, his children, and his neighbors. And to hear about how he continues to experience God day-by-day.

CHAPTER 17

A Seat at the Table

One day, I showed up at the dining facility later than usual. There were several casualties that day, so I spent a lot of time in the medical clinic, and also with two units who'd lost some Soldiers. I was tired and hungry, and finding an empty seat was difficult because several visiting units were at our FOB to assist with the operation, and many of the Soldiers were in the DFAC.

Finally locating a vacant chair, I placed my tray on the table. But, before I had a chance to sit, a Master Sergeant next to the empty seat growled in my direction, "No officers welcome here."

Obviously, the guy couldn't keep me from sitting there. He had no authority here, and clearly, I outranked him. I doubt that he noticed the cross on my uniform. He probably just saw the Major insignia on my chest, but it might not have made a difference even if he had recognized that I was a chaplain.

A lot of NCO's and officers don't like each other, don't respect each other. It's like there's an invisible barrier keeping us apart. But this guy had an aggressive attitude. Maybe because of the war; maybe because of something that happened in the past. There were three possible Courses of Action (COA), and I had to make a quick decision.

COA #1: Look for a different chair

COA #2: Attempt to pull rank

COA #3: Tell him I am an Honorary NCO

After completing a really quick SWOT analysis, I came to attention, turned up my collar to reveal a Sergeant E-5 insignia, and shouted as loud as I could, "Request permission to sit at your table, Master Sergeant," then remained standing at attention and waited.

The growler did a double-take, and his eyes got real big. "Have a seat, Sarge."

The other NCO's at the table were howling with laughter by now. They knew the Master Sergeant, but they didn't know me. And they had never seen a Major with NCO rank under the collar. They found the whole encounter to be quite entertaining.

After the others at the table calmed down, the slightly embarrassed and flabbergasted Master Sergeant said, "OK. S'pose you tell me why you're wearing that rank."

"Sure, Master Sergeant. When I was a rookie fresh out of Officer Basic, my first assignment was with a medical unit, where I had a great rapport with the NCO's. When they invited me to their Dining In at the end of the year, I thought it was because they wanted me to do the invocation, but that wasn't it. During the program, the First Sergeant pinned the NCO insignia on me, gave me a certificate, and appointed me to the honorary rank of Sergeant, making me an E-5 for Life."

"Hmmm. And you actually wear it?"

"Yes."

I wore the SGT Stripes invisibly throughout my career. When in the woodland Battle Dress Uniform, it was pinned under my collar. When we switched to the Army Combat Uniform, it was velcroed under the collar. And when I wore the Class A uniform or the Dress Blues, it was under the pocket flap, beneath my name. Every time I went to a new unit, I met with the First Sergeant or Sergeant Major, presented the documentation, and asked for permission to wear the rank and be part of the NCO corps. I was always welcomed.

Those Sergeant stripes were under the collar when I went outside the wire with the MiTT. They accompanied me every time I visited wounded Soldiers at the medical clinic. I wore them at each memorial ceremony or funeral. They were there for the worship services, the counseling appointments, and the Critical Incident Stress Management sessions. Whenever we had incoming rockets or mortars and we gathered in the bunkers … yep, still had them with me.

The day after I met the Master Sergeant in the DFAC, he showed up in my office. The night before, he was feisty and energetic; now he seemed sad and tired. Something had happened.

"Good afternoon, Master Sergeant. What can I do for you?"

"This morning, I lost a Soldier … a close friend. I wanted to know if you'd do a memorial ceremony tomorrow morning before we head out."

"Of course, I will."

"And Chaps, I'm sorry about last night."

"Not a problem, Master Sergeant. I understand."

"You can sit at my table any time."

It meant a lot that this senior NCO welcomed me at his table, that he wanted me to be there to honor his friend, and that we had overcome the invisible barrier between officer and NCO.

CHAPTER 18

Silhouette Man

Late one night, I was walking down the aisle between two rows of our housing containers. The camouflage netting overhead was eight feet above the ground, connecting the two rows of hooches, giving it the appearance of an indoor hallway. Out of my peripheral vision, I could barely see the outline of a man sitting on the steps in front of his door.

I was returning to my hooch dog-tired. I'd been to the medical clinic several times to visit that day's wounded. I'd visited three or four work areas to encourage, counsel, or pray, depending on what the people needed. In and out of bunkers several times. It was a hot and dirty day, and the last thing I wanted was to get into another conversation. My aim was to go inside, lock the door, fall on my bed, and turn off the world for a few hours. Forget brushing my teeth and showering. Maybe tomorrow. But what caught my eye in the moonless night was the orange, circular tip of a lit cigarette.

I greeted the silhouette. "How's it going?"

A voice behind the glow responded. "Survived another day."

"Sometimes that's all we can ask for," I mumbled.

I unlocked my door, walked inside, turned on the light, dropped my body armor and helmet onto the floor, turned out the light, and crashed-landed on the bed. Almost asleep, I heard a knock. Being in that not-quite-asleep-but-not-quite-awake nether world, I wasn't sure whether there was someone at the door, or if I was already dreaming. When I heard it again, I got up, opened the door, and saw the silhouette with the cigarette.

"Are you the chaplain?"

"Yes."

"Can we talk?"

I felt like saying, "C'mon dude. Give me a break." Instead, what came out of my mouth was, "Sure. Let me get some sandals on and I'll be right out."

I sat on the stoop across the hall as he lit up another cigarette and asked, "Mind if I smoke?"

I grinned, assuming he couldn't see my face any better than I could see his. I figured he was going to light up no matter what, so I said, "Nope. Go ahead."

The average smoker spends five-and-a-half minutes per cigarette, and the next time Silhouette Man spoke, he was on his fourth Marlboro. I wondered if he knew I had fallen asleep two or three times. It had to be past two in the morning.

"My name's Mac."

Not being able to see what he was wearing, I couldn't tell if he was a civilian or a soldier. "Hi, Mac. I'm Paul. What are you doing here?"

"I'm a cop from Philadelphia. Retired a few years ago. When the war started, the Army put word out that they needed experienced police officers to help train the IP (Iraqi Police). My old department notified me is how I found out about it. So, I thought, hey, why not? I'm bored staying at home by myself. Divorced. Daughter away at Princeton. I was a good cop, had done some training of younger, new guys, so why not? The money's good. And if I survive, just might have some stories to tell my grandkids someday. If my daughter ever has kids, that is. Where are you from, Chaplain?"

"From San Diego, but currently stationed in Atlanta." Did he really want to chat in the middle of the night?

"I was a cop for thirty years and saw some pretty interesting things." He paused for half-a-cigarette. "But for the first time in my life, I'm scared."

"What's happening?"

"We have two shifts. Early and late; I'm on the late shift, working from two in the afternoon til about midnight every day. Plus an hour to get there and an hour back. We go into town to the police station to teach the IP how to do their jobs. We send people to all the stations. I think there are about thirty IP stations in Diwaniyah. Most of our team is Army MPs, but there are a few civilian cops on each team. Most of us retired."

He lit another cigarette and continued.

"The station where I work is a two-story building surrounded by those huge apartment buildings–fifteen, twenty stories tall. The break area at the IP station is on the rooftop. You know how the men will drive over to the field on their way to work or during lunch or on their way home and shoot off the mortars?"

"Yeah."

"They do that to us with rifles. They sit up in those apartments like snipers, waiting for one of us to be visible in a window, or when we go out on the roof for a break, and they start firing at us. We're trapped. We've been shot at every day the past three weeks.

"This afternoon I was on the roof. It had been a pretty quiet day until a little after four when the shooting started. I dove for the parapet that surrounds the rooftop patio, using the wall to protect myself. The two guys next to me were killed. One American cop like me, retired, from Cincinnati, I think. One Iraqi. Several downstairs in the main part of the building were shot, too. Injured; none killed down there. I felt so powerless, so defenseless. We're like helpless lambs waiting for the slaughter. It's starting to get to me."

I hurt for this faceless guy from Philadelphia. I wanted to move over, sit next to him, and put an arm around him, but then I thought that might seem weird to a total stranger, especially a career policeman. Maybe after we got to know each other I'd have that opportunity. So I asked him a question. "Mac, what time do you return to Echo after your shift?"

"It's usually a little after 1:00. 1:30, maybe."

"Would it be helpful for me to be here when you get back, so you have someone to talk to about what you just went through?"

"Yeah. I think it would. I'd like that."

I started waiting up for Mac most nights, letting him set the agenda for what we talked about. He'd tell me about his day, and I'd tell him about mine. He was proud of his daughter, what she was studying, and her career plans; I was proud of my sons and what they were doing. We talked about what we wanted to do after we got home from Iraq. He liked working again, liked the money, and wondered if there might be other jobs for retired cops somewhere. He was checking into it, and coming up with some intriguing possibilities. My wife was getting ready to move down to Florida for a new job, and I was hoping for a transfer to be down there with her. I was already checking into it.

Mac and I usually talked for about an hour, sometimes two. He always called me Paul and I called him Mac, but midway through the second week of these middle-of-the-night rendezvous, he said, "Hey, Chaplain, I have a question for you."

"What's on your mind, Officer?"

"I grew up going to church occasionally, and I've always wondered about something. Where do they get those stories about Jesus?"

"What stories are you talking about, Mac?"

"You know. Jesus walking on the water. Turning water into wine. Stories like that."

"Those stories come from the Bible."

"Really?"

"Yeah, really."

The Philadelphia Cop puffed on his cigarette a few times, thinking. "Do you think you could get a Bible for me?"

"Yeah, wait here." I went and got a Bible from my hooch and handed it to him.

"Thanks."

"You're welcome. I'll talk to you when you get back tomorrow night."

"You mean, if I get back!"

"Yes, if you get back. But I have a feeling you'll be OK."

The next night I waited for Mac, but he didn't come. The next two nights he wasn't there. Worried about him, I went over to our Police Transition Team (PiTT) headquarters, and found out he'd been staying in town the past few nights. Things had become so dangerous, that instead of walking out of the police station at midnight and risk getting shot, he took a cot and slept at the IP station. The fourth night, he returned at his normal time.

"I've missed you, Mac."

"I missed you too. And our talks," he said. "Tell you what. I haven't had a shower in four days. I'm taking the next two days off. How 'bout if we meet for lunch tomorrow. Right now, I just want to take a shower and crash on my bed."

"I understand. Sounds good to me."

When I saw Mac in the DFAC the next day, it was the first time I had seen him during daylight hours, so I finally got to see what he looked like. A slender 6'1", short, curly black hair, thin-line mustache and goatee. Italian ancestry. I finally got to put my arm around him and give him a hug. We went through the buffet line to get our food, then sat down across from each other. He had slept late, and the lunch crowd had come and gone, leaving a relatively quiet place to talk.

"Thanks for the Bible, Paul."

"You're welcome, Mac."

"So that's where the preachers get all those stories about Jesus! I thought they made them up. I read the whole New Testament in three days."

"No way!" I was quite surprised he read all of it in three days.

"I did. Now I know for myself. I feel like I have insider knowledge about Jesus, Peter, and the rest of the apostles. I don't have to take someone else's word for it anymore."

"What do you think about Jesus, Mac?"

"Well, I see him in a whole new light. If what I read is true, then he really was God who became a man. Is that right?"

"That's the way I read it, Mac."

"And the point of Christianity isn't about going to mass or church or doing the sacraments? It's about having a relationship with the Lord?"

"I can't think of a better way of saying it. Going to church and participating in the sacraments can help us, they can encourage us, and they can teach us, but if we miss the part about having a personal relationship with Jesus Christ, then we missed the main point. The most important part. In fact, a pastor friend of mine in Salt Lake City says it this way, *Christianity isn't a religion. It's a relationship.* That's when it's real. That's when it's personal. That's when it's powerful and life-changing. And that's when it moves beyond arguing or debating about God, to loving God and loving people whether or not they believe the same way we do, because the point of genuine Christianity is recognizing that God is love. He loves us, and empowers us to love other people."

Mac sat there. Thinking. Eating. And then, "I feel something happening inside. Something strange, something fresh. What is it?"

"Well, I can only guess. But I'd say you're probably ...."

"I think I know," he was getting excited and wanted to be the one to say it. "For the first time in my life, I feel God in me. Like I have real faith. Not just going through the motions. Not just doing it because the priest or the pastor or the chaplain told me what to do."

He stopped again. Took a sip of his coffee. Then asked, "How do you pray?"

"Praying is simply talking to God about what you're going through. What you're thinking or feeling. Or what you're concerned about. You can talk to God the same way you talk to anyone. In church we sometimes say things a bit different because, well, because he's God, and we're ordinary men, and it's a ceremony type of event. But you don't have to say it any different. You just tell the Lord what you're thinking and feeling."

The Philadelphia Cop looked at his watch. We'd been talking almost two hours when a mortar landed about a block away. Sirens blared immediately. We grabbed our gear and ran outside and into the bunker. There were seven or eight others already there. "Can we finish later tonight?" Mac asked.

"Yes. I've got to go over to the clinic once the all clear sounds. And I've got some other stuff to do. What time?"

"Normal time?"

"Wait. You're taking two days off and you want to talk at one in the morning? I was hoping I'd get a bit more sleep tonight," I chided.

"Yeah, I know. But I want my body clock to be ready when I go back to work, so I sort of want to get back on schedule."

"OK. One o'clock it is. See you tonight."

I hurried over to the clinic. After visiting the injured and talking with the medical team, I went over to brief the commander. While reporting what had happened and giving him the stats, I asked if he was doing OK.

"Chaps. I need to get out of here. Pray for me."

The Colonel was not a religious man. That's the closest he ever came to talking about God or religion or his own need. Most likely, he was just expressing his own pain, frustration, and desire to get out of the Middle East, rather than truly asking for prayer. Who knows? Maybe he was being sincere. I told him I would pray, and I did.

That night I attended a Bible study in the conference room of one of the Border Transition Teams (BiTT). A handful of men were there. Doc, the medic who earlier had the shakes, led worship with his guitar. It was good to see he was still doing well.

The BiTT commander was my friend, Steve. He led the prayer and discussion that night.

I asked the men if they would join me in praying for the chief surgeon, who was walking toward the medical clinic when a mortar landed about ten feet away. Shrapnel shredded his right arm and the side of his chest. We prayed for the post commander, and a cop named Mac. This particular BiTT team was going out on patrol first thing the next morning, so they asked me to pray for them.

After the meeting ended, we stayed another hour just to talk, tell a few jokes, and take some pictures. On one wall there was an American flag next to an Iraqi flag. We got a picture of Steve and me standing in front of those flags.

"Steve, I need to ask for a couple of favors." At that point he was a Lieutenant Colonel and I was a Major.

"Sure, what do you need?"

"I just got notice that my promotion to Lieutenant Colonel is official, and I'd like to know if you would officiate at my promotion ceremony."

"I'd be honored to do that," he answered. "When is it? I'll be gone a week, you know."

"How about a day or two after you get back?"

"You got it. What's the other thing?"

"Because I'm being promoted, my MiTT commander can't be my rater. He's a Major and I'll become a Lieutenant Colonel. I need someone here who outranks me to write my evaluation when I'm done and it's time to leave. Since you have date of rank on me, and you know the work I've been doing here at Camp Echo, I was wondering if you could do that."

"Let me check with my boss and with MNC-I, and get back to you. "

"Fair enough. Thanks. Stay safe out there. I'll be praying for you."

I went back to my hooch, read for an hour while listening to some music, and waited for Mac to knock on my door. When he did, I went out to finish our conversation. He picked up right where we left off when the mortar interrupted our afternoon.

"I feel something stirring inside of me," he told me. "And I want you to pray with me. I don't know when it's going to be my turn to die, but for the first time in my life, after reading the Bible this week, I think I finally get what Jesus is all about."

"All right," I said. "You pray the way I told you earlier, and then I'll pray."

He didn't need me to pray. He did a great job of it all by himself. He told the Lord what he was going through, what he was feeling, and asked God to forgive him of his sins and give him a fresh start in his life and in his faith. When he finished, he looked at me and said, "I feel good inside. I feel clean."

"That's a great feeling, isn't it?" Then I prayed for him.

"How do I tell my daughter about this? With my past, I don't think she'll understand."

"I think you just tell her the truth, Mac. Keep it simple. Be honest."

"I haven't always been the best father to her."

"All the more reason to keep it simple and honest. Don't try to force your experience on her. Just be genuine. When are you going to see her?"

"She graduates on June 5, and I'm hoping to use my two weeks R&R so I can be there."

"Take some time each day to read your Bible and pray. Trust the Lord to guide you in your relationship with your daughter, and he will help you."

"I can do that," as he pulled out his lighter and another cigarette.

I got up and started to walk to my hooch.

"Hey, chaplain."

I stopped and looked at the silhouette. "Yes?"

"Thanks."

CHAPTER 19

Safest Place in Iraq

Seventy-three miles from Camp Echo is the old city of Babylon. During the Old Testament Babylonian exile, Daniel was thrown into the lion's den because he prayed three times a day to his God. But the Lord protected him, which meant that the pit full of hungry lions turned out to be a pretty safe place for him. Not a single one of those ferocious beasts took a bite out of him. Instead, they lay down and purred.

Babylon was also where Shadrach, Meshach, and Abednego were thrown into a fiery furnace because they refused to bow down and worship a golden statue. Boldly they declared, *If the God we serve exists, then He can rescue us from the furnace of blazing fire, and He can rescue us from the power of you, the king. But even if He does not rescue us, we want you as king to know that we will not serve your gods or worship the gold statue you set up.*

Their faith was remarkable, and didn't depend on whether they escaped. They were fully prepared to risk everything, which meant they didn't serve the Lord only during the good times. They didn't trust God only to get their way. There was nothing selfish about their prayer, their life, or their religion. Their faith in God was genuine, even when it resulted in persecution. Even when it meant risking their lives. Death was certain, and they knew it ... unless God did a miracle. Either way, they were determined to be faithful.

According to the narrative in the book of Daniel, the fire was so hot that the soldiers escorting them to the flames died on the spot. Yet, not only did Shadrach, Meshach, and Abednego survive . . . not a hair on their head or their arms was singed, and not a thread of their clothing burned. Apparently, they never even felt the heat. It was like they were taking a walk in the park on a cool, breezy day.

When the smoke cleared, King Nebuchadnezzar looked into the furnace, and to his amazement, there was a fourth man standing with them in the fire. The king couldn't believe his eyes. Daniel 3:25 tells us that Nebuchadnezzar exclaimed, *"Look! I see four men, not tied, walking around in the fire unharmed; and the fourth looks like a son of the gods."*

Daniel understood the dangers of breaking the law and praying to his God. Hungry lions can easily tear a man apart. Shadrach, Meshach, and Abednego knew the risks when they made up their minds not to bow to the king's golden statue.

It just so happened that an angel of the Lord closed the lions' mouths, and Daniel survived to tell the King once more about the goodness and the reality of the true God. It turned out that for Shadrach, Meshach, and Abednego, the safest place in Babylon was right there in the middle of the blazing heat. Why? Because that's where God wanted them to be. And because that's where that fourth man was going to be . . . In the fire!

In the New Testament, the eleventh chapter of Hebrews makes it unmistakably clear that not everyone who takes the risk of faith will escape pain or death. I would encourage you to read the entire chapter, but verses 32–38 show how the situations turned out for some of God's people.

|||||||||||||||||||||||||||||||||||||||||||||||||||||||||||||||||||||||||||||||||||||||||||||||||||||||||||||||||||||||||||

And what more can I say? Time is too short for me to tell about Gideon, Barak, Samson, Jephthah, David, Samuel, and the prophets, who by faith conquered kingdoms, administered justice, obtained promises, shut the mouths of lions, quenched the raging of fire, escaped the edge of the sword, gained strength after being weak, became mighty in battle, and put foreign armies to flight. Women received their dead—they were raised to life again. Some men were tortured, not accepting release, so that they might gain a better resurrection, and others experienced mockings and scourgings, as well as bonds and imprisonment. They were stoned, they were sawed in two, they died by the sword, they wandered about in sheepskins, in goatskins, destitute, afflicted, and mistreated. The world was not worthy of them.

|||||||||||||||||||||||||||||||||||||||||||||||||||||||||||||||||||||||||||||||||||||||||||||||||||||||||||||||||||||||||||

Being a disciple of Jesus Christ always involves risk. Some will face ridicule. Others might lose their jobs. Some are abandoned by their family. Others experience physical torture. Some will survive; others may die. What is God asking you to risk?

In every situation mentioned in Hebrews chapter eleven, the dangers were real. Some escaped and some didn't. Some survived, while others died. The bottom line is that your faith will cost you something. There are risks to being a person of faith, and God is calling you to accept the challenge, count the cost, and take the risk.

Danny the Interpreter knew what his friends and family would do to him once they found out he had become a Christian, but knowing Jesus personally was worth more than any potential danger or pain. Christians in many places around the world are experiencing persecution at this moment. In the same way, it might cost you something to follow Jesus. Whatever that might be, is it worth it? Only you can answer that.

It turned out for me that the safest place in Iraq was right there at Camp Echo, on the outskirts of Diwaniyah. Not because of our Army. Not because of the Coalition Forces. And not because of luck. No, the safest place for me was smack dab in the middle of God's will, right where the Lord called me to be, doing exactly what he called me to do. Even if I had been hurt, being in the center of God's will is what matters.

I understood the risks, but I went to Iraq because I believed it was part of God's plan. I could have lost my arm or leg or sight. I could have lost everything. My wife could have lost her husband, my sons their father, and my grandchildren their grandfather.

But like those men in the book of Daniel, I was determined to be faithful regardless of the outcome. What I discovered after I got there, was that the fourth man in the fire was going to be there, too, making Camp Echo the *Safest Place in Iraq*.

Epilogue:
Before & After

CHAPTER 20

Getting to Iraq

I wasn't supposed to go to Iraq. In fact, the career track I was on as an Active Duty chaplain in the Army Reserve was as a trainer/supervisor/administrator. Additional duties included Force Management, Operations, and Budgeting, but definitely not deploying or going to war … until I asked.

In December 2006, one month after my son returned from a year in Iraq with the Army's 4th Infantry Division, the US Army Forces Command sent a Request for Forces to the Army Reserve headquarters in Atlanta, where I worked. They needed three Army Reserve chaplains to fill an immediate shortage in places where there were no chaplains, and it would take months before the Regular Army could put chaplains in those spots.

I was part of a team that trained and supervised Army Reserve chaplains nationwide. We conducted regional and national conferences for our Reserve chaplains and Chaplain Assistants. The key word was *Readiness*. We never knew when or where Big Army would need another Unit Ministry Team (UMT), so Army Reserve and National Guard chaplains had to be in a constant state of readiness.

During the decade following the terrorist attacks of September 11, 2001, the normal deployment cycle made every Army Reserve and National Guard unit vulnerable to being deployed every three years. But every part-timer also knew he or she could be called up "out of cycle," depending on the war and the needs of the Army. Those of us who were part of the Full-Time Support staff made sure the *Weekend Warriors* were ready when needed, but we were hardly ever the ones who went overseas.

Whenever a Request for Forces came to our office, my boss had to determine which Army Reserve chaplain would fill the mission. We often discussed these matters during our weekly staff meetings. He and I had gone to officer basic training together, and had remained friends after we graduated and went our separate ways. Now, sixteen years later, it was an honor to work at headquarters, and even better to work with my friend.

When the tasker arrived indicating that a chaplain was needed at Camp Echo, I said to him, "Sir, I'd like to go. I've trained a lot of our chaplain teams before sending them over. I'd really like to do some of that war-time ministry myself, get a taste of what our troops are going through, see if I can make a difference, and then be better prepared for training our chaplains to go overseas."

He dismissed the idea right away. "No, I need you here."

I wanted to tell him that I sensed a calling from God, that it seemed the Holy Spirit had put this idea in my head, that I had prayed about it and talked about it with my wife, and we agreed this was probably the Lord's will. But the Army doesn't always listen to that kind of talk, even among chaplains. Army Reserve policy was for part-time Reserve chaplains to deploy, and for Full-Time Support chaplains to remain in the states. The problem, however, was the shortage of chaplains, and we were running out of people to send.

Another factor was that the Army Reserve was in the middle of a three-year reorganization, and my job as the Force Management chaplain was to recommend the appropriate rank and unit location of the chaplain positions. Building the structure to make sure we had chaplains in the right places was an important part of ensuring the religious freedom guaranteed by our Constitution; providing the counseling our soldiers and their families needed; advising the commander and command staff regarding morale, religion, and ethics; offering suicide awareness and prevention training; and doing a whole lot of things that only the chaplains do in the military.

But he was adamant. "We can't afford to miss this opportunity to place our chaplains where they're needed most, and you're the expert. You're the only chaplain with the appropriate training, so there's nobody else who can do that. You're staying here. We'll find someone else to go to Iraq."

The next day I went to his office to beg and plead. I was prepared to grovel, too. Instead, I came up with a different approach. "Sir, do you remember the memo that came out last week about deployment being one of the top criteria for future promotions?"

"Yes. I read it."

"Do you think I'm doing a good job for you?"

"Sure, why are you asking that?"

"Here's why. On one hand you tell me that I'm doing great. That you like my work and that I'm a good chaplain."

"It's true. What are you getting at?

"And now the memo comes out stating that promotion boards will only consider Reserve officers who have deployment experience. The bottom line is that your decision to keep me here because you need me in this project will end up hurting my chances for future promotions. I won't be competitive."

The Colonel sat back in his chair. "I see your point."

"All I'm asking," I continued, "is that you think about it before you send someone else."

"OK. I'll think about it. But I'm not making any promises."

"Thank you."

The next day, he called me to his office. "I've thought about what you said, and it makes sense. Plus, all of our Reserve commands are being asked to make sacrifices, sending people, and being short-handed, so I'm willing to make a sacrifice, too. I'll let you go. But here's the deal. If you go to Iraq, here are the terms. I don't want you gone more than six months. And one more thing . . ." There was a long pause as we stared at each other.

"What's the other stipulation?"

"You have to take your Blackberry and your laptop so you can stay in touch and keep up with your work here while you're in Iraq."

"Are you kidding me?" I found it hard to believe that he would ask me to do both jobs.

"That's the only way I'll agree to let you go. So, if you're convinced this is God's plan for you, then go for it. Just make sure we stay on track to get the Force Management approvals that we need."

My boss knew what he was doing. He understood what was going on in the Army Reserve Transformation, and couldn't afford to miss the opportunity to ensure that the emerging force structure contained the appropriate authorizations for Chaplains and Chaplain Assistants. Yet, as he stated, he was also aware of the deployment cycle. Every Army Reserve command was struggling because of manpower demands and drains. He saw a much bigger picture than I did, and he was right. As a leader, his responsibility was to make sure the entire job got done, and if that meant he had to say "no" to me, he was prepared to do that . . . even though we were friends. He also had me cornered ideologically. If I thought this opportunity truly was from God, then I should be willing to count the cost, sacrifice, and work twice as hard to make it happen.

"OK. I'll do both jobs. And you can instruct the personnel section to include the clause on the orders, *No more than 180 days*. I'll take the Blackberry and the laptop. And I'll let the Force Management guys on the third floor know that I'll be working from a remote location for the next few months, and that I'll continue to provide input on your behalf."

"Agreed," my boss declared. "When you get there, I want you to check in by phone at the start and at the end of each week, and I want a weekly report on your Force Management work here in Atlanta. I can't afford for us to fall behind."

"Yes, sir."

In January 2007, when my boss said he'd let me go to Iraq, the pastor of the church that Linda and I were attending, Trinity Church in Sharpsburg, GA, had asked the entire congregation to fast one day a week during the month of January, as a way to start the new year with a spiritual focus. We signed up to fast on Wednesdays that month. When I got orders to go to Iraq, I decided to continue fasting one day a week throughout the deployment. I am confident that making the sacrifice to fast and pray helped prepare me emotionally and spiritually for what I was to experience in Iraq.

In addition to prayer and fasting, I selected a daily devotional book by Henry and Richard Blackaby, *Experiencing God Day-By-Day*, for my personal reading and the basis for my Sunday preaching. This was another significant aspect of staying prepared emotionally and spiritually during the war, and helped me discern what God was doing in the lives of the men and women I served.

I didn't know what to expect when I got to Iraq. Even though I had been well-trained as a chaplain, and even though I had trained more than a hundred other chaplains and sent them into battle with their units, being there in person was a different ballgame. Circumstances, people, and conditions make each situation unique. The training and discipline are essential, but you have to add your own instinct and discernment, and in a sense, fly by the seat of your pants, figuring it out as you go. Sometimes you simply do what the manual or the SOP says to do. Other times you have to be creative, stepping out in faith to accomplish the mission, staying "prayed up" and trusting God each step of the way.

Either way, I felt like I was ready, and up to the challenges ahead. I managed to keep up with my work in Atlanta while, at the same time, ministering in Iraq. Having the Blackberry and laptop made it possible, because I was able to be in touch any time I needed to.

The stories I shared in this book are true, and are presented to the best of my recollection. I included some of the names of people in the stories, but I changed most names, and others I left nameless to protect their privacy. If they read it, they may recognize themselves. But whether they reveal themselves as the people in the events is up to them.

Together, we experienced the atrocities of war, but also some powerful answers to prayer. I hope you are encouraged and inspired by reading about what the Lord did at Camp Echo, outside of Diwaniyah, in South Central Iraq.

CHAPTER 21

Setting Up Shop

The Blackhawk flight from Baghdad down to Camp Echo took about two hours, a gunner at each side door keeping an eye on potential attacks from the ground. They wore night vision devices, and I didn't, so I wasn't able to see what they saw, but two or three times during the ride they fired their machine guns. I thought I heard some gunfire from down there in the dark, but our helicopter wasn't hit.

It was just past midnight when we landed. We threw our gear onto the ground, jumped out, and the chopper took off, leaving us standing there in the moonless night. We had no idea where we were, no clue where we were supposed to go.

Night in the Iraqi desert was darker than I expected. There was no ambient light like we'd get in almost any town back in the States. I couldn't see a thing: not the ground in front of me, not my assistant. I reached blindly for one of my bags, found the one I needed, and using the Braille method, located my flashlight. We were still lost, but at least we could see the ground, each other, and the wall around the perimeter of our new FOB.

"Let's go this way," the Master Sergeant said.

"OK. Sounds good." I don't know how she knew which way to go, but a good officer knows to trust an NCO's instincts.

We left our stuff where the helicopter dropped us and walked. After what seemed to be a quarter of a mile, we saw a solitary, dim light bulb up ahead. "That's gotta be the Flight Operations Center," MSG France announced. We introduced ourselves to the two soldiers manning the small office.

"We heard you'd be coming. Welcome to Camp Echo. Go get your luggage or whatever you brought with you, and we'll get you a ride."

In the pitch-black night, we managed to find our way back to our personal belongings, supplies, literature, and the equipment we needed if we were going to stay in the desert six months. It took three trips to carry our stuff from the landing pad to the Flight Ops Center. Each round trip was a half mile, so including the first hike to find the Flight Ops Center, we made that trek four times in the dark, three times carrying our stuff. The boxes and trunks were heavy, so I had to haul most of it, and it wasn't easy. Remember, I was fifty-two years of age, not the young soldier I used to be! By the time we finished, we'd walked almost two miles. Finally, having retrieved everything, we plopped on the ground to rest and wait for the truck.

We discovered that everyone at Camp Echo was on edge. But then, war is like that. Stress, fear, heat, loss of friends and co-workers, and not enough sleep work together to create a tense environment. "Welcome to your new home-away-from-home."

The pre-fab units we were housed in were like metal storage crates. At least they were air conditioned, and most of the time the A/C worked, which was good because the temperature averaged between 110 and 120 degrees during the day.

Each crate was designed for two persons, and we were told that the Master Sergeant and I would be sharing a hooch. When I mentioned that it wouldn't be appropriate for us to live in the same room because one of us was male and the other female, the housing manager told me there was no other option. "Since you came in as a small two-man unit, you have to be housed together. That's the policy. Plus, there's a shortage of units."

A soldier away from home, far from spouse or partner, faces sexual temptations, and too often, gives in to them. Sexual needs and desires are powerful. Matched with opportunity, what seems fun at the time can lead to sexually transmitted disease, divorce, unwanted pregnancy, or all of the above. I wouldn't say sexual promiscuity at Camp Echo was rampant, but it certainly wasn't rare.

War breaks people. Some are broken physically or psychologically, while others are broken spiritually, morally, or relationally. We are not the same after the war as we were going in. That's why the military tries its best to provide the kind of support our people need. Chaplains, psychologists, doctors and nurses, lawyers, financial advisors, and physical therapists are some of the support staff available. We also encourage our people to develop mentor relationships, and many do. But when we are far from home for long periods of time, and in extremely difficult circumstances, sometimes personal values are pushed aside, and we do things that we wouldn't have thought ourselves likely to do.

I've had my share of temptations and weaknesses, but I went to Iraq determined not to be among the military personnel who have sex while away from home. I wanted to be sexually and spiritually faithful to my wife and to the Lord. You've heard the expression, "What happens in Vegas, stays in Vegas." Our soldiers rephrased it to, "What happens in Iraq stays in Iraq."

But I don't subscribe to that mentality, so I told the housing manager, "Look. We're not a *two-man unit*. One of us is a female. I'm the new chaplain here. How would it look for me to be living with my female assistant?" Besides, I need a place where I can meet privately with people for counseling.

"Sorry, Chaps. It ain't gonna happen. You can't have a place of your own."

"Then pair me with another guy."

"There isn't anybody else, and there's no other available hooch."

No matter what I said, I couldn't get him to understand. So, I made a decision he didn't like. "Fine. I'll be sleeping outside on the ground," I told him.

"You can't do that."

"I'm not asking; I'm telling you. Pair me with another guy, or give me a place by myself. Justify it however you want to. Let me use it as an office or a place for counseling, a storage facility for the supplies and equipment I brought with me, whatever. But I will not share a room with a female. I'll find a spot outside and put my sleeping bag on the ground."

"You have to get the commander's permission for single occupancy."

"Then call him. That's your job, isn't it?" He wasn't used to having someone yell at him, and to be honest, I don't yell at people very often. This was one of those times.

We stared at each other, wondering who would back down. I couldn't believe we were even having this conversation.

"Fine. I'll assign her to another hooch," he snarled.

"Thank you." Later we would become friends, but not that day.

MSG France and I located our hooches and moved our stuff in. We spent most of the first day unpacking and arranging our stuff. In my room were a single bed and a lockable metal closet. On the wall at the far end was an air conditioner. The only decoration I brought was a picture of my wife. I had the place to myself the entire time I was at Camp Echo. Home sweet home.

The next item on our agenda was to find an office, so the following day. My assistant and I went around meeting people, asking if they had a spare room we could use. Most military bases designate a space for the chaplain, but in the three years Camp Echo had been in operation, there hadn't been a chaplain, so there was no place for us. Our job was to set up a new program and get it up and running, so we needed to find office space, get it connected with phones and internet, and then decide where to have worship services. By mid-afternoon of day two, we stumbled upon a building that was unlocked, and appeared to be unoccupied.

"What do you think?" I asked.

"I think it'll work, but we need to find out whose building it is," said the Master Sergeant.

It was a simple, straight wood-frame building with plywood walls, no insulation, and a wooden floor raised about twenty inches off the ground. A hall ran down the middle of the building with a double wooden door at each end. Offices lined both sides of the hall, four on each side, and in the middle of the building was a single restroom. The inside walls were painted a dirty off-white, the outside a dirty off-beige. The floor was a cheap brown tile that was always covered with sand and dust no matter how recently it was swept. Although nobody was in the building at the time, some of the rooms had office furniture and phones.

MSG France went to find out who "owned" the building, and I sat behind one of the desks to rest. I picked up the phone, and discovered that it worked. "This would be a nice office," I half thought, half prayed. It wasn't much, but considering what we had to work with, we could make it do.

France returned forty-five minutes later. "It belongs to KBR."

"What's KBR?" I asked.

"It's a civilian company based in Texas that has a contract to provide most of the civilian workers here. Apparently, the guys who work in this building are out looking for parts or supplies, and will return sometime tonight."

"Good work, Master Sergeant. I think I'll write a note and tape it to the door, asking if we can use one or two of the rooms for our offices."

The next afternoon, we returned to the building and found two men. The guy in charge was a fifty-eight-year-old guy from Louisiana, named Bob. The other was a U.S. Air Force First Lieutenant. Twenty-three years old, he was the military finance liaison who oversaw KBR's funding and projects.

After we introduced ourselves, Bob said, "Hey, Chaplain. The LT and I found your note. We think it'd be fine for you guys to use two of the offices down the hall by the door. Temporarily, though. Depends on whether any more of our people come. If so, they'd have priority, and you'd have to move out."

"We understand. Thank you."

"Oh, one problem, though," the Lieutenant said. "There's no phone or internet in those rooms. You'll have to check with IT to see if they can install them for you."

"I'll take care of that," answered MSG France. My Chaplain Assistant could do anything, and she did everything well.

She promptly walked the quarter mile to the IT building and requested the installation. "No problem, Master Sergeant. We'll get right on it. Can prob'ly get it done about two days from now."

Two days later, a young tech Specialist arrived with wires and tools to get us connected to the internet. "We'll get you online by the end of the day."

Four hours later, he told us he was done. Packed up his tools, and left. I plugged in the laptop, connected the phone line, tried to get online . . . nothing. It didn't work.

So, the next day the Specialist returned and worked on it some more, concluding that it already worked. He and I got into an argument, yelling at each other. Finally, he turned and walked out, and went back to the IT building, leaving me standing there next to a computer that couldn't access the internet.

I was so angry, I stomped over to his boss's office and told the supervisor that his guy did a lousy job and it didn't work. I wanted someone ASAP who knew how to do the job. Then I returned to the office. I was mad. I had only been at the FOB a couple of days, and had already yelled at people twice: first the housing manager who wanted me to share a room with my female Chaplain Assistant, and now the young IT technician. Shouting at people isn't a good habit for anyone to get into, especially a chaplain.

I turned off the computer, restarted it, and when it came back on, I tried to get online one more time. This time it worked. You gotta be kidding. You mean, the guy I'd been yelling at and accusing of doing a lousy job … he was right?

I was embarrassed, and knew I was wrong. Slowly I returned to the IT shop and knocked on the supervisor's door. "Excuse me," I started. "I need to apologize to you and the Specialist."

"For what?" He was still upset and didn't want to talk to me.

When I told him the story, that the internet and phone worked, and that his guy had completed the job correctly, he asked one of his guys to go get the young man who had done the installation. He didn't look very happy to see me.

"I came back over to apologize to you and to your boss for the things I said, and for accusing you of not doing the job right. You were right, and I was wrong. Please forgive me."

He broke into a grin that covered his entire face. "No officer ever apologized to me before. And plenty of 'em been wrong. You're the first one to ever come back and admit it. Tell you what, if I ever feel like going to church, I'll go to a church where the chaplain is humble enough to say he's sorry."

Throughout the day, mortars or rockets exploded somewhere at Camp Echo, which meant any task, conversation, or meeting could be interrupted without warning, and we'd all head for the nearest bunker.

By the end of our first week at Camp Echo, MSG France and I had moved into our hooches, located an office, got internet and phone hooked up, found a place to conduct worship services, and managed to dodge all the incoming rockets and mortars. We'd also met most of the key leaders in the various agencies and offices, which was important for gaining access when we needed to visit people. We worked long hours, and since we didn't have a vehicle, we had to walk wherever we went. It was always hot, and it wasn't an easy job, but we were getting it done.

Master Sergeant Rosita France was a great Chaplain Assistant. She was personable and people liked her. She cared about them. People started coming to our religious services because she befriended them or invited them. And being a senior NCO, she knew how to get things done, how to work the system.

She was also important to me personally, because there were periodic warnings from our intelligence people that Camp Echo might be invaded by terrorists. We were ordered to wear our Kevlar helmets and vests and to keep our weapons with us at all times. But American chaplains are non-combatants. I didn't have a weapon. If I found one or was given one, I wasn't allowed to use it. This is a matter of U.S. law, military regulation and policy, and international treaty. That's one of the reasons every chaplain has a Chaplain Assistant. They can carry weapons, and they'd better be able to shoot.

At 9:45 p.m. on Friday night, one week after we arrived, several mortars exploded. As soon as we heard the signal allowing us to leave the bunker, MSG France and I went over to the medical clinic. The front entrance had a long ramp allowing access to wheeled carts and gurneys, but we usually approached from the rear of the building. In a hurry to check on casualties inside the clinic, we walked around and hopped onto the side of the ramp. Even though my vest weighed more than thirty-five pounds with the armor plates inserted, and the helmet added another four pounds, I made it onto the ramp and started to enter the clinic.

MSG France wasn't so lucky. Though she had made that jump many times a day for the past week, this time the weight of the armor, combined with her being tired at the end of the day, proved too much. She didn't quite jump high enough, fell forward, and landed on her left arm, shattering her elbow. Being a strong, dedicated soldier, she got up, grimaced, and continued working. The next day she went back to the clinic to have a doctor examine her elbow. She returned to the office, her arm in a sling. It was bad enough that she was in pain. Now she had to turn in her M-16. An injury like hers prevented her from being able to carry a weapon because she couldn't shoot. And she was supposed to be my force protection.

Before long, she was on a flight home, having been at Camp Echo less than three weeks. Her elbow needed surgery that couldn't be done at Camp Echo, and probably months of healing and physical therapy. The Military Transition Team (MiTT) that we were assigned to told me that since I no longer had a Chaplain Assistant, they would provide the force protection I needed. That meant a lot to me.

The rest of the time I was there, I would be without a Chaplain Assistant. MSG France had done a great job getting us set up, so I was able to minister effectively after she left. And as you've already read, the Lord provided several other people to form a fantastic ministry team. More importantly, the Holy Spirit began showing me what he was planning to do in the lives of the people at Camp Echo.

After ninety-two days in the desert, I returned to the States, and the Army provided a full-time chaplain who would be at Camp Echo a lot longer. My job was done, and as the apostle says in 1 Timothy 4:7, I had fought the good fight, I had finished the race, and I had kept the faith.

Chapter 22

CNN and the Miami Herald

When I returned to work at the United States Army Reserve Command in Atlanta, GA, I made a list of eighteen experiences I wanted to tell the Bible study group, many of the same stories that are included in this book. I took a stack of 3x5 cards, wrote the title of one story on each card, numbered them one through eighteen, and took the deck of cards up to the third floor of our building to the conference room where we met every Tuesday for a "Brown Bag Lunch and Bible Study."

Placing the cards on the table I told the group what they were, and suggested that anyone may come take a card. Then, when we started the discussion, they could read what's on the card, and I'd tell the story. It took longer than an hour, and we all had to get back to work, so we finished the stories the following Tuesday.

It was a fun way to share with them what I had experienced and what God had done while I was in Iraq. They got to rejoice with me and praise the Lord for his goodness and faithfulness. And, it led to some fascinating discussions over the next few months.

Because of the article I had written for my denominational magazine, and because my boss had sent it to the Public Affairs Office, when I got back to the States, quite a few people had heard about some of the things that happened. I was invited to speak at several churches and military events. And, of course, my wife wanted to know everything.

At the same time, I started experiencing worse symptoms of PTSD. I couldn't sleep. I had nightmares and dreams that were so real I would wake up thinking I was still in Iraq. If I heard thunder or a noise like a car backfiring, or someone slamming a door, I would flinch, wondering where my helmet was. Because of the mortars and rockets at Camp Echo, I got into the habit of eating extremely fast. We had to be ready to run to the nearest bunker without notice. To this day, I have a tough time lingering over a meal, even on a date with my wife. Daily life and routines were boring in comparison to being in the war.

I'd always been a happy person, but I wasn't happy, now. When unhappiness lasts too long, it morphs into discouragement. Discouragement that sticks around becomes depression. And, persistent depression changes you. I had that kind of depression for more than a year. Part of it was because my wife and I were living in Atlanta, but she took a teaching position down in Florida, and moved a month after I got home. I was then dealing with the post-war thoughts and emotions without a wife to come home to at the end of a workday.

In March of 2008, a couple of weeks before Easter, I got a phone call from Phil Long, a reporter who covered Central Florida for the Miami Herald. He wanted to interview a Christian soldier who had been in Iraq the previous Easter, and write an article comparing Easter in Iraq with Easter at home in the States. We agreed to get together at my home in Florida the next time I was visiting my wife.

The interview process was like a conversation between friends. Phil and I had a great time getting acquainted, and quickly developed a good rapport. He took a few pictures. We talked and laughed, and hit it off personally. So much, in fact, that my wife and I drove to Vero Beach to see him and his wife a few months later. His piece, which ran on Saturday, March 22, 2008, the day before Easter, started as follows:

||||||||||||||||||||||||||||||||||||||||||||||||||||||||||||||||||||||||||||||||||||||||||||||||||||||||||

Last Easter ... Chaplain Paul Linzey ministered to troops as hell rained from the heavens exploding near his chapel. Within hours of his homily on Christ's resurrection, Linzey had given last rites to one soldier, and nursed the wounded souls hurt in the afternoon mortar attack at Camp Echo near Ad Diwaniyah, 100 miles south of Baghdad.

||||||||||||||||||||||||||||||||||||||||||||||||||||||||||||||||||||||||||||||||||||||||||||||||||||||||||

Meeting with Phil for the interview was fun. I was able to relive some of the stories from my time in Iraq, and then frame them in a positive way so that it became therapeutic for me personally.

The day after the interview with Phil was Easter Sunday. CNN had called the Public Affairs Officer at Fort McPherson a few months prior to ask about interviewing someone who had been in Iraq the previous year. The PAO, being a friend of mine, asked if

I'd be willing to do the interview. When I said I would, he coached me on what to say and what not to say.

"A lot of reporters will try to trip you up or catch you off guard in order to get you to say something you didn't really intend to say. So be careful," the media officer warned. "Know your message, stick to it, and have fun."

CNN had sent some sample questions. They, too, said they wanted to focus on the contrasts of Easter in Iraq while there's a war going on, with Easter in America where it's peaceful.

I told him I was willing to do the interview, but that I'd be down in Florida with my wife for Easter. When he mentioned this to CNN, they made arrangements for a limo to pick us up from our home, drive us to the television studio, and then take us home afterwards. Linda and I talked during the forty-five-minute drive to Tampa as if this sort of thing happened all the time. The whole experience was a lot of fun for Linda and me. They made us feel like celebrities, not just because of the limo ride, but they treated us special at the studio, too.

The Limo took us to downtown Tampa, where I would be interviewed live at a television studio; the interviewer himself was at CNN in Atlanta, and I could see him on a large screen. The limo arrived at 6:00 in the morning. The interview was at 7:30.

T.J. Holmes and Betty Nguyen were the morning co-hosts for the show called *Sunday Morning: Faces of Faith*. Like a typical talk show format, they covered more than a dozen stories before they finally got around to pointing at me and saying, "Are you ready? Four, three, two, one. You're on."

During the interview, they showed five or six photos of Camp Echo that I had provided. T.J. Holmes conducted the interview, beginning as expected. What follows is the exact transcript from the CNN broadcast, including the inaccuracies.

|||||||||||||||||||||||||||||||||||||||||||||||||||||||||||||||||||||||||||||||||||||||||||||||||||||||||

HOLMES: We're going to turn to Easter last year in Iraq. After a quiet morning worship service there was a sudden attack on a U.S. military unit. One soldier killed, five injured and in times of crises like this, soldiers depend, of course, oftentimes on their faith. And in this particular case they turn to Chaplain Paul Linzey. Chaplain Paul Linzey joins us now from Tampa. Chaplain Linzey, we appreciate you this morning. What are your thoughts waking up on this Easter as opposed to what you have gone through last Easter?

LT. COL. PAUL LINZEY, CHAPLAIN, U.S. ARMY: There's a big difference from last year, waking up every morning to explosions of rockets or mortars. It's a lot more peaceful here.

HOLMES: And sir, why did you volunteer in the first place to go to Iraq?

LINZEY: Because I love soldiers. I love people and I feel that I could be of help and encouragement to them.

HOLMES: Sir, what did you find? Last year you might have seen this, an article on in "Newsweek," talking about chaplains and the struggles that they have in administrating to these soldiers in Iraq. And they wrote so eloquently, "God can be lost or found in a fox hole but rarely does war leave someone's faith untouched." How was your faith touched by the Iraq war?

LINZEY: It served to deepen me. It served to connect better with our soldiers but also connect better with people who are going through crisis or struggles of their own. When you see people at the point of crisis, you can see them at their best or their worst. And so, I've had appreciation for what people are going through.

HOLMES: You say yours was deepened. In this particular "Newsweek" article I'm talking about was actually about a chaplain who lost his faith. A deeply, devout man who actually lost his faith in the Iraq war. Did you really never find yourself questioning your faith and your god?

||||||||||||||||||||||||||||||||||||||||||||||||||||||||||||||||||||||||||||||||||||||||||||||||||||||||||||||||||||||||||||||||||||||

The rest of the interview veered away from what CNN had said they wanted to discuss. Instead, T.J. tried to get me to admit that my faith was shaken because of serving in Iraq during the war. I had read the *Newsweek* article, and later I would read the book he wrote about his experiences and his spiritual journey. He really did come close to forsaking his faith in God because of the atrocities he witnessed, the pain, the suffering, the inhumanity of war. But his book also discusses his faith being restored, and the end of the story is that his relationship with God was intact.

T.J. sounded incredulous that I didn't question my faith, and pressed the point several times. He finally moved on to another topic, before asking, "What are you doing this Easter."

I was surprised by the questions T.J. threw at me. I wanted to tell my story. I had practiced how and what I would say. Instead, he wanted to talk about something else entirely. I was angry. I felt ambushed. I felt like I had failed. I felt that my opportunity to celebrate what God had done was ruined by T.J. Holmes' decision to change the subject and talk instead about people who lose their faith when going through a time of struggle, instead of those who turn towards God. Added to that, was my inability to think on my feet. I felt like a fool.

The evidence indicates that a lot of people turn towards the Lord in times of crisis. Many Soldiers discover their need for God during war. That's what was happening at Camp Echo while I was there. Another dynamic is the fact that most chaplains are well-trained, professional clergy who have a lot of pastoral experience before becoming a military chaplain. Then, the Chief of Chaplains and the Chaplain School train us even more, so we are well-prepared to help others during the tough times. Most of us don't turn our back on God when the going gets tough.

I received calls and emails from friends and family around the country who sided with me. "What was that guy's problem? Who does he think he is?"

However, when I look back at the video or the transcript of the interview now, I see it in a different light. T.J. actually did a great job focusing on some poignant issues facing not only soldiers in wartime, but issues facing anyone when life is at its worst. The fact is, a lot of people do question whether there is a God. Or they wonder, "If there is a God, why doesn't he stop the madness, the suffering, the horribleness we too often see in the world?"

I have found that the Lord makes a huge difference internally, even though he might not always intervene in the external circumstances. There are times when God breaks into our lives with the bold, the preposterous, or the incredible. Some of the experiences I had in Iraq are like that. Most of the time, however, the Lord makes his biggest impact on the inner being of the person who trusts in him.

It has been my privilege to see it, feel it, hear it, touch it, and taste it from both sides–internally and externally. I have seen him do the audacious miracle, and I've felt him stirring gently, almost imperceptibly, deep down inside. As Dr. Blackaby suggests, "We ought to live each day with tremendous anticipation as we look

QUESTIONS AND TOPICS FOR DISCUSSION

1. When the housing officer told Chaplain Linzey that he'd have to share a room with his female assistant, was Linzey's response appropriate? Is there a better way he could have handled the situation?

2. Have you ever been told a situation would be totally safe, only to discover that it wasn't? How did you feel when you realized it wasn't safe after all?

3. Chaplain Linzey says it's important for all God's people to be involved in ministry. How have you been involved in ministry? What ways might you want to serve in ministry in the future?

4. The captain in the Ukrainian army, said God healed his eyes. How does that fit with your understanding of miracles or answered prayer?

5. Where do you like to go for personal conversation? Do you feel more "at home" in a church, a home, a park, a coffee shop, or a different place? Explain the reasons why.

6. In your opinion, should Christians serve in the military? Why or why not?

7. The author mentions several ways he heard from God. Can you identify some of them? How does God speak to you?

8. After being in the Hummer that caught on fire, Doc experienced fear that wouldn't stop. Chaplain Linzey talked about his father's fear during WWII, and about his own fear at Camp Echo. When have you experienced fear that you couldn't shake?

9. Does being in God's will guarantee safety? Does it mean you're exempt from getting hurt?

10. What is God asking you to risk in order to follow Christ?

11. The author told about the interview where he felt the CNN guy tripped him up by asking questions he wasn't expecting and wasn't prepared for. Have you ever felt you were verbally ambushed, and that you didn't know what to say? What was it like?

12. Was there ever a time in your life when you weren't sure God was real? Have you ever felt like you were losing your faith in God? What happened? How long did it last? Was your faith eventually restored?

13. What's it like to be shot at? To be attacked? How might that change a person?

14. Chaplain Linzey's mentor told him "friendship follows ministry." How might you apply this philosophy of ministry where you live or work?

15. How would you describe a "ministry of presence"? How does it differ from other forms of ministry?

16. What do you think the author wants his readers to take away from this reading experience?

GLOSSARY

AIT   Advanced Individual Training. Right after Basic Training, soldiers go to another military school to learn the specific skills of their chosen career path, or Military Occupational Specialty (MOS).

Battle Rattle   The body armor, helmet, and other gear our soldiers wear for protection.

BiTT   Border Transition Team. American Army units that assist the Iraqi forces in patrolling and controlling illicit border crossings on Iraq's international borders. Specifically, these teams focus on assisting the DBE in preventing infiltration of insurgent, terrorist, and criminal elements into Iraq.

Bunker   A concrete shelter to protect from mortars and rockets. The bunkers at Camp Echo were about ten feet long, four feet tall and wide, open at both ends, with a bench inside.

Camp Echo — Many of the Forward Operating Bases were identified by a letter instead of having a name. "Echo" is the word for the letter "E" in the military alphabet. Since I was at Camp Echo, it's safe to assume there were also camps called Alpha, Beta, Charlie, and Delta. Maybe even a Foxtrot and a Golf.

CISM — Critical Incident Stress Management. A specialized method of helping people who have been traumatized.

COL — Colonel

Diwaniyah — The large city near Camp Echo is pronounced "dee-wuh-kneé-yuh."

DFAC — Dining Facility

Dining In — A formal dinner event only for the members of a military unit.

Dining Out — A formal dinner event that spouses or guests are invited to.

Eye-in-the-Sky — A drone with camera or heat sensors.

FOB — Forward Operating Base

Hooch	The metal housing unit we lived in. Similar in appearance to a metal cargo crate hauled by semis or stacked on ships, it's also called a Tin Can or Containerized Housing Unit (CHU).
IA	Iraqi Army
IP	Iraqi Police
IED	Improvised Explosive Device. There are many different kinds.
KBR	The contracting company that provided civilian workers in Iraq. KBR used to mean Kellogg, Brown, and Root but now it just means KBR.
T-wall	Twelve-feet-high concrete wall placed around the FOB perimeter, and around some of the buildings inside the FOB. They protect from gunfire and shrapnel.
M-16	The basic rifle issued to soldiers.
MiTT	Military Transition Team. American Army units that spend time with and train the Iraqi military units.
MNC-I	Multi-National Corp, Iraq.

MND-CS	Multi-National Division, Center South. One level down from MNC-I.
MOS	Military Occupational Specialty, a specific job in the military
MRE	Meal, Ready-to-Eat. Prepackaged food.
MSG	Master Sergeant. Every rank in the Army is abbreviated to three letters or digits.
MWR	Morale, Welfare, and Recreation: the combination gym and entertainment center at Camp Echo.
NCO	Non-Commissioned Officer. Sergeants, soldiers from the ranks E-5 to E-9.
NCOIC	Non-Commissioned Officer In Charge. The highest-ranking NCO in a unit.
Officers	First Lieutenant (1LT), Second Lieutenant (2LT), Captain (CPT),Major (MAJ), Lieutenant Colonel (LTC), Colonel (COL).
Outside the Wire	Off-post, outside of the safety of the FOB's concrete walls.
PiTT	Police Transition Team. Military and civilian police officers who trained the Iraqi police in law enforcement strategies and tactics.

R & R

Rest and Recreation. During a 12-month deployment, many soldiers were allowed to go home for two weeks about half-way through the year.

Soldier

A member of the Unites States Army. People in the Air Force, Navy, Coast Guard, and Marines are never called "soldiers." People in the Air Force are airmen. Those in the Navy are sailors. Marines are called Marines. And people in the Coast Guard are called Coasties or Coast Guardsmen.

SWOT

A SWOT analysis is a compilation of your Strengths, Weaknesses, Opportunities and Threats. It's used in business and in the military in strategizing and making decisions. It comes in handy on a personal level, too.

Terp

Interpreter. During operations in other nations, the military hires locals to serve as interpreters or translators for our interaction with host nation military and political leaders.

UMT

Unit Ministry Team. Consists of at least one chaplain and one NCO. Sometimes the term Religious Support Team (RST) is used.

ABOUT THE AUTHOR

A native of Southern California, Paul Linzey was a pastor before going into the Army chaplaincy. Retiring at the rank of Colonel, he now devotes his time to writing, mentoring, and teaching . . . when he's not traveling with his wife.

Dr. Linzey graduated from Vanguard University in Costa Mesa, CA, with a major in biblical studies. He completed the Master of Divinity at Fuller Theological Seminary, the Doctor of Ministry in Pastoral Skills at Gordon-Conwell Theological Seminary, and an MFA in Creative Writing at the University of Tampa.

Linzey is an adjunct professor and a mentor in the Doctor of Ministry program at Southeastern University, Lakeland, FL, and a guest speaker for conferences, churches, and military organizations. He is a mentor for clergy and lay leaders of many denominations. His focus is often on marriage, parenting, leadership, discipleship, and small group ministry. He has provided pastoral counseling to many couples and individuals.

He served as an editor and writer for *The Warriors Bible*, released in 2014 by Life Publishers. His first book, titled *WisdomBuilt Biblical Principles of Marriage*, was published in 2019. *Safest Place in Iraq* won a first place Peach Award in the *Bible Studies & Nonfiction* category at the 2019 North Georgia Christian Writers Conference Competition. Then it won a first place Gold Award at the Florida Writers Association's Royal Palms Literary Award Competition for 2019. Linzey freelances for several magazines. Each week he works on a blog, a chapter of a book, and a new article.

Interests include music, digital photography, movies and theater, sports, travel, and family. He and his wife have three adult sons, ten grandchildren, and a Beagle.

His theme Scripture is First Thessalonians 2:8, "We loved you so much that we were willing to share with you not only the gospel of God but our lives as well, because you had become so dear to us."

Paul Linzey may be contacted at https://paullinzey.com.

ALSO BY PAUL LINZEY

A companion volume for *Safest Place in Iraq*, this study guide presents questions and discussion prompts for further reflection

about ministry, military chaplaincy, the Bible, and relationships. Perfect for small group discussion or classroom use, as well.

Linzey's first book shows couples how to build a great marriage, and provides congregational leaders a practical plan for helping the couples in their care.

The result is an easy-to-follow book that may be used in couples classes, sermon series, seminars, or retreats. It may be used in counseling and private conversations, or by the couples themselves. WisdomBuilt Biblical Principles of Marriage presents twelve principles for a joyful, fulfilling marriage.

https://paullinzey.com/books

The Warriors Bible contains an easy-to-understand introduction for each book of the Bible, several indexes, plus 50 longer articles for the warrior.

Paul Linzey wrote twenty-five of the call outs, and edited more than one hundred call outs and articles. Scott McChrystal was the Managing Editor, guiding the project from inception to completion.

Paul Linzey is a freelancer who has written for more than a dozen military and religious print and online magazines, and has a poem in a poetry journal. He is also a blogger. Many of his articles may be read at https://paullinzey.com.

ACKNOWLEDGMENTS

There are a lot of people who played a part in making this book happen, and a lot of people I need to say "thank you" to.

First is my wife, Linda Linzey. Yes, the same person who "always wants to know more about everything." Without her agreement, I wouldn't have asked to deploy. But she prayed about it and felt that it was what the Lord wanted me (us) to do. Thanks also for praying for me every single day. You are an amazing wife and spiritual partner.

My boss at the US Army Reserve Command was Colonel Ron Casteel. We completed the Officer Basic Course together, kept in touch through the years, and then had the opportunity to work together in Atlanta. Ron, thanks for your faithful mentoring and guidance throughout my Army career. And for letting me go to Iraq . . . even if for no more than 180 days! Without you, there is no story to tell.

Every military chaplain is required to have an ecclesiastical endorsing agent. Mine was Colonel Scott McChrystal, who had been an Army chaplain before working at denominational headquarters. I had met Scott at the United States Military

Academy at West Point when he was a chaplain there, and my son was a cadet. Scott, your leadership and support were fantastic, and I am especially grateful for the Church Connection Program that you headed up. That was what led me to ask several congregations for their prayer and support when I deployed.

Those pastors and their congregations prayed regularly for me. They sent cookies, popcorn, and other goodies. They mailed Sunday worship services on CDs, made sure I had reading material to give to the troops, and provided office equipment that the military wasn't able to provide. These pastors and the wonderful people in the churches made a huge impact for me and Camp Echo. I couldn't have asked for a better support system. The four pastors and their churches were:

Dr. Mark Anthony, Trinity Church in Sharpsburg, GA

Rev. Jim Ayers, Life Church in West Valley City, UT

Rev. Gene Linzey, Christian Family Church in Taos, NM

Rev. Jack LaPietra, New Life in Christ Church in Lakewood, CO

My son, now Lieutenant Colonel Kevin Linzey, was a Captain in Iraq as an Infantry officer the year before I went over. Kevin, you shared your deployment experiences, encouraged me to "go where soldiers go," and prayed for me and the ministry at Camp Echo. You even gave me the MP3 player you listened to in Iraq. I used it every day in my room, and also plugged it into the sound system and used it to lead worship whenever I didn't have a guitarist. I appreciate you, Son.

When I went to Iraq, I was part of a six-person team: three chaplains and three Chaplain Assistants. When we got to Iraq, we ended up going three different places, but we trained and traveled together on the way. One of the other chaplains was Dan White, a Presbyterian chaplain who told me one day, "I just have a feeling we're going to see miracles, that God is going to do some fantastic things while we're over there." Before you told me that, Dan, I hadn't really thought about, prayed for, or expected miraculous experiences. But hearing you say that, got me thinking and praying and believing that extraordinary events could and would actually happen. Through you, the Lord elevated my faith and my expectations.

Master Sergeant Rosita France, my Chaplain Assistant, ministry partner, and friend . . . thank you so much for your excellence, your professionalism, and for always being really good at Situational Awareness. You are a significant reason why things went so well at Camp Echo, even after you left. I want to thank you for grabbing me by the collar that day, and pulling me back inside when I started to run for the bunker without my helmet on. My friend, you saved my life.

While preparing to deploy, I began reading the devotional book *Experiencing God Day-by-Day*, co-written by Dr. Richard Blackaby and Dr. Henry Blackaby. Thank you, Richard, for making the book available to our military personnel, and for the many ways God used that book to strengthen me and prepare me for what I needed to do. Thanks also for agreeing to write the Foreword for this book. You are a tremendous servant of the Lord, and an asset to the Kingdom of God.

John Capouya, Don Merrill, and Josip Novakovich were my mentors at the University of Tampa when I completed the Master of Fine Arts in Creative Writing. I started writing these stories while in their workshops, and the first version of *Safest Place in Iraq* was my thesis under the guidance of John Capouya. John, Don, and Josip: you taught me, shaped my writing, and kept pressing me to let go of my bad tendencies as a writer. Thank you.

After editing the manuscript a few times, I posted a note on Facebook, asking for volunteers who would read the book and offer criticism for improvement. You are the ones who helped polish the manuscript by providing outstanding perspective and feedback. Wow, I am grateful to you all. The truth of the matter is, you guys prevented a few major embarrassments because of the goofs, foibles, and errors you detected: David Hall, Greg Thomas, J.D. Wininger, Steve Langehough, and several others. Ron Casteel, Mike DuCharme, and Chris Linzey provided key insights, as did Carl Colbert, Daphne Tarango, and the Lakeland Christian Writers Group. Truly a team effort!

In the front of the book, you can see the names of the people who wrote an endorsement. This group includes pastors, chaplains, authors, and military chaplain endorsers. Thank you for believing in me and the message of this book.

I want to thank Mr. Terry Whalin & the Morgan James Publishing team. I met Terry three years ago at a Florida Writers Association one-day event in Orlando, and instantly liked the guy. The next year, he was a guest presenter at a writers conference I conducted at Southeastern University in Lakeland, FL. Thank you, Terry, for your encouragement and guidance in bringing this project to fruition.

And finally, I want to thank Ms. Tiffany Gibson, for her expertise as project manager, and for shepherding the book step by step through the process to the finished product.

9 781642 799170